Enterprise Supply Chain Management

Enterprise Supply Chain Management

Integrating Best-in-Class Processes

VIVEK SEHGAL

WILEY

John Wiley & Sons, Inc.

Published by John Wiley & Sons, Inc., Hoboken, New Jersey.
Published simultaneously in Canada.

For general information on our other products and services, or technical support, please contact our Customer Care Department within the United States at 800-762-2974, outside the United States at 317-572-3993 or fax 317-572-4002.

Wiley also publishes its books in a variety of electronic formats. Some content that appears in print may not be available in electronic books.
For more information about Wiley products, visit our web site at www.wiley.com.

Library of Congress Cataloging-in-Publication Data:

Sehgal, Vivek.
   Enterprise supply chain management : integrating best in class processes / Vivek Sehgal.
       p. cm.
   Includes index.
   ISBN 978-0-470-46545-5 (cloth)
   1. Business logistics. I. Title.
   HD38.5.S44 2009
   658.5–dc22

                                                                    2009005643

Printed in the United States of America

10 9 8 7 6 5 4 3 2 1

To my parents

Contents

Preface

When I started my career in supply chain more than a decade ago, it was still an emerging field. There were very few books in the marketplace on supply chains, no courses being taught, and most companies were just learning about the new opportunities supply chain management could provide them. The solution providers were similarly trying to define the space and simultaneously establish their thought leadership in the process. For most people in general, supply chains were a mystery, and I remember the difficulty in explaining to my fellow travelers on my frequent consulting trips about what I do for a living.

Enterprise resource planning (ERP) solution vendors had been offering their master resource planning (MRP) based scheduling solutions for some time, primarily targeted at manufacturers; distribution resource planning (DRP) evolved for retailers, which was similar in concept to MRP but adapted itself to more distribution-intensive planning.

Today, it is clear that supply chains are here to stay. Most companies have established supply chain organizations, and supply chain solutions have matured into well-integrated suites of applications. However, most books on supply chain are still either focused on the science (such as forecasting) behind supply chain applications or specialize in a very narrowly defined area such as warehousing or transportation. These approaches leave out the big picture and deprive prospective students and practitioners of an overall understanding of the scope that supply chains cover and how they fit into the enterprise.

It was with the intention of providing the bigger picture that I started to put together this book. The objective is to provide a high-level understanding of all supply chain areas and establish the relationships among them. The book covers these processes in a generic fashion without any specific industry vertical in mind. The basic concepts of supply chain management are similar and apply to all industry verticals with some variations. The examples provided are sometimes specific to an industry; this is simply to provide the most relevant example while describing a function. This book does not go into a deeper specialized discussion on any specific function or solution but otherwise covers a wide scope of supply chain functions in the enterprise.

Of course, generalizing such a vast area always poses challenges. There are several variations of every concept when it is deployed in practice; the terms used are not quite standard across the industry. Also, relative organization of business processes and their subfunctions is always debatable. I have pushed ahead with generalizing when possible, defining industry terms where relevant, and providing context for organizing the functions together as I thought fit. Practicing readers may find it organized a little differently from what they have seen elsewhere, so I wanted to establish my methodology up front.

The objective of this book is to provide an appreciation for the supply chain management functions for the enterprise. While specific industries have different challenges, there are common supply chain concepts and processes that run across the industry spectrum. I believe that understanding these supply chain processes offers an opportunity across industries to evaluate their current supply chain practices and leverage the best-in-class concepts to their own challenges.

Supply chain management as a discipline primarily evolved to manage the flow of material required to support the business of the enterprise. The business, therefore, dictates the characteristics of such flow. For example, supply chains for the manufacturing industries address the flow of material during the buy, make, distribute, and sell processes, while retail industries might not care much about the "make" operations. Whereas both verticals in the example require executing the buy, distribute, and sell processes, these processes differ among the different industries. However, the underlying concepts, the reasons to establish and execute a process, the questions that a process addresses, and the data inputs and outputs of these processes remain closely related across all industry verticals.

Therefore, this book looks at supply chain processes from an enterprise point of view, and describes the underlying concept for a specific process, what it achieves, and how it is generally executed. I have intentionally kept these descriptions generic, though I have used examples to point out the most relevant differences among prominent industry verticals.

Manufacturing industries typically have large asset investments in manufacturing facilities and skilled resources. These industries may also have substantial inventories in raw materials and work-in-progress to support their manufacturing operations. Therefore, the prominent themes for a manufacturing supply chain are establishing the optimal product mix through good demand planning, managing raw material supplies for consistent production runs, and managing the assets, resources, and inventories for optimal utilization. The manufacturing supply chains typically have a smaller footprint of items and facilities, and a more manageable network. However, creating an optimal manufacturing plan that simultaneously constrains on available material, resources, and process sequence is among the hardest problems to solve even with the recent advances made in mathematical modeling of such situations. The variations in the manufacturing business models pose their own challenges to understand the best supply chain practices. Contract manufacturing, which has become very popular in the high-tech sector, has very different challenges compared with traditional manufacturing, and there are differences to consider among different types of manufacturing activities, such as discrete versus process, and make to order versus make to stock.

Retail supply chains also differ from the supply chains in other verticals. They are distribution intensive. They can be highly seasonal in nature. They typically do not model hard capacity constraints, though they can benefit from such modeling. And multi-echelon planning is still in its infancy in the retail vertical.

Retailers also have other challenges in dealing with supply chain problems due to their extremely large volumes of master and transactional data. Depending on the retailer's specialty, it can carry as much as a quarter-million products for sale with thousands of retail locations spread all over the world, and an equally large distribution network with tens of distribution centers. An average retailer also deals with thousands of suppliers that may be supplying the merchandise from an equally diverse number of locations. Add them up, and you are looking at an extremely large supply chain network with thousands of nodes and thousands of routes to optimize and manage.

I have also included some related topics at the end of the book in the appendices. These subjects are important to the practitioner from the point of view of general appreciation and awareness. Appendix A covers the subject of technology. Technology plays an important part in supply chain processes. It provides automation as well as decision-making capabilities through modeling and optimization of complex business scenarios. There are many options, and this appendix provides a quick overview for selecting and managing these technology deployments and the consequent organizational changes. Appendix B presents an overview of radio frequency identification (RFID) in the industry. While this technology has been around for some time, and shows considerable promise, it has not yet been widely adopted. This appendix summarizes the capabilities and looks at the possible reasons for low industry adoption. Appendix C discusses cross-docking as a supply chain strategy. It has been widely popular in recent years. However, it is a complex process and needs elaborate evaluation of current processes and attendant systems for successful deployment. Appendix D presents the relationship between the supply chain and finance. Supply chains closely affect the financial efficiency of corporations, and understanding how these operations affect the higher-level financial metrics establishes the foundation for making a successful case for supply chain initiatives. Appendix E is my attempt at predicting the future of supply chain processes. There is great awareness of the impact of human activity on the environment, and efforts are underway to develop business practices that are more environmentally friendly. I believe that supply chain processes will also evolve to align with this new world order, driven through legislation, or corporate fervor, or both. This appendix is an attempt at describing that logical evolution of supply chain management processes in years to come. Appendix F is a list of commonly used EDI transaction sets, and the last, Appendix G, provides an overview of the global trade terms from the International Chamber of Commerce.

Supply chain management has its unique challenges for all industries. If these challenges are understood and appreciated in advance, it can make supply chain transformations more predictable, productive, and manageable.

The target audience for this book is primarily corporate supply chain managers in business and IT who may or may not have an academic background in supply chain management. Supply chain students and the occasional practitioner may find this useful as well to learn about underlying concepts, processes, efficiencies, and metrics. The supply chain courses are relatively new offerings and most corporate managers have had to learn about supply chains on the job; this book is designed to help them in this endeavor. The book is intentionally written with no specific bias toward business or IT and covers both aspects where it makes sense. For example, most supply chain processes today are managed through technology solutions that are highly mathematical in nature. Understanding the theory of how physical supply chain elements are modeled in these solutions without going into the depths of mathematical modeling definitely provides business folks with a deeper appreciation of the solutions. By the same measure, their IT counterparts will do well to understand what exactly these processes provide to the business, how they impact a-day-in-the-life scenarios for the practitioners, and what metrics they impact.

The scope of supply chains is continuously emerging and expanding functionally, technologically, and geographically. This adds to the challenge of keeping up to date with the latest while simultaneously juggling the current problems that corporate supply chains face. For the purposes of keeping this book to a focused discussion, we have defined our own scope that we will treat as the core supply chain functions.

Acknowledgments

I am thankful to many people for helping me in this endeavor: to my guide and mentor, Pervinder Johar, for his comments and feedback; to Karen Etzkorn, one of the most charismatic leaders I have had the opportunity to learn from; to Yasser Alkazzaz, for his feedback and support throughout the project; and to Randy Hill, a friend and colleague, for his unbridled enthusiasm.

Enterprise Supply Chain Management

PART I

Introduction

CHAPTER 1

What Is a Supply Chain?

Various definitions abound for *supply chain*. These definitions change with the industry vertical and the context. We will stick to a generic definition that defines *supply chain* as the *flow and management of resources across the enterprise for the purpose of maintaining the business operations profitably*. This really is an extremely generic definition, and therefore may be fuzzy at first, but we will examine the components of the definition, and a picture of a supply chain will soon emerge.

Definitions

Resources in this definition can be materials, people, information, money, or any other such resources that must be managed for profitable business operations.

Materials can be raw materials, work-in-progress (WIP), or finished products. In the context of retail industries, it is the merchandise that the retailers sell. It costs to buy this merchandise, store it, and distribute it. If a store is out of merchandise, it loses the sale, thus affecting revenue; if it is overstocked, it increases the inventory, affecting operating cash flow negatively. Some of this merchandise may be seasonal, and therefore must be planned based on seasonal patterns. It may be local (e.g., folding portable chairs with your favorite team's logo on the back), may depend on weather (e.g., snow boots and jackets), or may need to be custom ordered (e.g., purple carpet). All these factors make the merchandise a resource to be managed. This illustrates the "right-time, right-place, right-quantity" mantra that you may have heard in relation to supply chain management.

People can also become constraints that must be managed for profitable operations. In a supply chain context for retailers, think of the distribution center associates that must be available to receive and ship all the planned merchandise from a warehouse in a given day. For manufacturers, this relates to the direct labor.

Management of the flow of *information* is equally important to smooth operations. Extending the distribution center example, if the information on inbound shipments to the warehouse is not visible to the warehouse manager, it can create problems for labor scheduling as well as downstream fulfillment planning for the store orders. In fact, visibility across supply chain functions that can provide a consolidated view of demand, inventories, and orders has emerged as one of the most important and valued functions in most companies.

Money is another resource. Often, the objective of a lot of supply chain planning and execution initiatives is to minimize the cost of doing business (or maximize the profitability).

Other resources can be physical assets such as buildings and machinery. Manufacturers routinely plan operations for their factories with the intent of maximizing the utilization of most critical assets. Retailers can sometimes find themselves in a fix when the number of trailers they manage falls short of the shipments they need to send to their stores, or when the warehouse capacity is too small for the inventory they must hold for ramping up to the holiday season.

Flow and management of these resources is key to supply chain management. Some of the resources actually flow through the supply chain, such as merchandise. It flows from the suppliers' warehouses to the retailer's warehouses, then to their stores or customers. Others help the flow of this merchandise, such as workers in the distribution center. Recall that the objective of a well-managed supply chain is to plan and execute the *flow and management* of the *resources* for the purpose of maintaining the business operations profitably. Recall also that the *resources* are generally scarce and cost money. Putting these two together, the emphasis on *profitability* becomes clear. If your supply chain can achieve this better than your competitor's, you are in good shape. If not, supply chain improvements can help.

Across the enterprise refers to the extended footprint of supply chain operations as it straddles the planning and execution processes across several functions. These processes cover planning processes like demand and supply planning, and then continue with the execution processes of purchasing, manufacturing, stocking, and distribution of inventory through a network of warehouses and transportation resources.

The final words in our definition refer to the *profitability*. Supply chain processes directly affect the costs of planning and operations, and therefore provide extraordinary opportunities to reduce the cost of goods sold (COGS) and improve asset turnover, thereby enhancing profitability of a corporation. A quick primer on how supply chain improvements affect the corporate finances is provided in Appendix D.

Physical Manifestation of a Supply Chain

Now that the definition in theory is behind us, let us look at the physical manifestation of supply chains. This is easier to understand with an example. We will look at a typical retailer with stores and warehouses; though some retailers, such as grocers, may also have manufacturing facilities as part of their supply chains. All retail supply chains have distribution-intensive operations irrespective of the specific retail segment they represent. Examples of these retail segments are soft-line retailers like apparel chains, hard-line retailers like home-improvement chains, or department stores.

Most retailers have brick-and-mortar stores where the merchandise is presented for the customers to buy. Some of the new-breed retailers (such as Amazon.com) may not have physical stores, but they do provide an environment where the merchandise and customers can interact. Physical or not, the stores fulfill the same function—they bring the merchandise and the customers together and provide an environment conducive to sales.

The merchandise arrives in the stores from the retailer's own warehouses, or directly from the supplier's warehouse. All of these (namely the store, retailer's warehouse, and the supplier's warehouse) together represent the physical supply chain.

As shown in Exhibit 1.1, if the *store* is in New Jersey, and the supplying *warehouse* in Florida, then the *merchandise* may be carried on a *truck* along *I-95*. The elements in italics represent respectively the *demand location*, *supplying location*, *product*, *transport resource*, and *route*. Together, all of these constitute elements of the supply chain that must be managed by the retailer to smoothly serve the customer.

When customers buy, the stores need to replenish the merchandise. This merchandise is typically replenished from the warehouses. But the warehouses themselves need to be replenished with merchandise from the vendors. That brings us to the *purchase orders* against which such merchandise is supplied by the vendors.

Before any purchases can be made, we need to establish the total customer demand, existing supplies, and remaining demand that must be fulfilled from new purchases. The purchase orders are therefore planned through a process that computes the demand for merchandise at each of the locations and predicts how much should be bought, where, and when. As these purchases must be made in advance of actual demand, the demand planning processes help in establishing the projected (forecast) demand, and merchandise planning processes establish assortments to decide what will be sold where. We will touch on all of these processes in the following chapters.

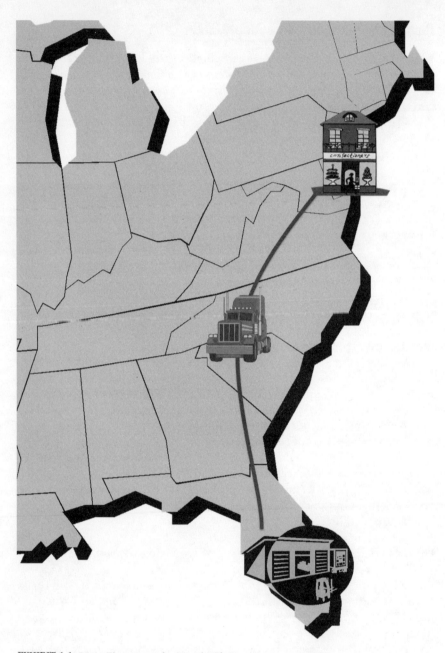

EXHIBIT 1.1 Basic Elements of a Supply Chain

Elements of a Supply Chain Model

Now that we have a fairly good idea about the physical components of a supply chain, let us look at how a typical supply chain is modeled to support the business processes. Supply chains have two ends: the demand end and the supply end.

The demand end of the supply chain models elements of the supply chain where the demand originates. Examples of the demand end are stores, a Web-storefront, or customers. Business requirements determine whether individual customers in a supply chain are modeled. For most retail operations catering to individuals, this may not be required; but think of a manufacturer with a wholesale operation and you might want to model the customers as well. Whether one models the stores at this end, or the end-customers, depends on the level at which a consistent demand pattern exists, which also can be easily modeled. For example, for a large retailer with thousands of stores and individual cash-and-carry customers, stores may be very well suited to model demand. However, for a consumer goods manufacturer like Procter & Gamble, large individual customers like Wal-Mart or Target will be better suited to model demand. We will also call this end of the supply chain the *downstream*. Exhibit 1.2 shows the demand and supply ends of a supply chain.

The supply end of a supply chain represents the sources of supply, such as suppliers' warehouses or a factory. These represent the supply chain elements that provide supplies to address the demand generated at the other end of the supply chain. We will call this end of the supply chain the *upstream*.

Thinking of the supply chain in terms of *demand end* and a *supply end* also helps in understanding one of the core problems that supply chains solve—that of balancing supplies against demand. Demand flows from downstream nodes to the upstream nodes in a supply chain network, while the supplies flow from the upstream nodes to the downstream nodes.

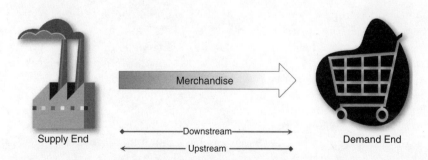

EXHIBIT 1.2 Demand and Supply Ends of a Supply Chain

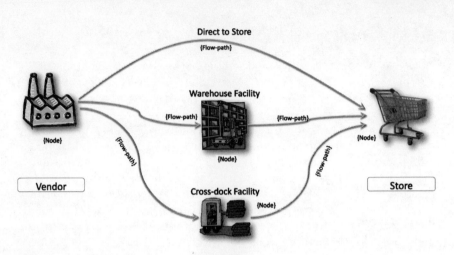

EXHIBIT 1.3 Supply Chain Nodes and Flow-paths

Between the supply and demand ends of a supply chain are modeled other elements that constitute the *distribution network*. Examples of these elements are warehouses, cross-docking facilities, transshipment points, processing facilities, assembly plants, and so on.

All the elements we have mentioned here are different *types* of locations. We will call them *nodes*. The relationships among these nodes are also modeled in a supply chain to establish the valid paths along which goods/services can travel. We will call these paths *flow-paths*.

As depicted in Exhibit 1.3, the network of nodes and flow-paths in the supply chain model creates the supply chain *network*. Though it may not be identical, the supply chain *network model* closely mirrors the physical supply chain for a retailer.

Attributes of a Supply Chain Node

A node in a supply chain model generally represents a type of location along with its inventory, operations, resources, skills, and any other attributes relevant to supply chain operations. Nodes add *value* to the material flowing through the supply chain. Exhibit 1.4 shows a supply chain node and the typical elements that can be defined at a node.

Nodes typically model locations. *Locations* can be used to represent a manufacturing location (such as a factory), distribution location (such as a warehouse), selling location (such as a store), or a supplying location (such as a vendor/warehouse). Locations can have multiple purposes as well. For example, a factory may also serve as a warehouse.

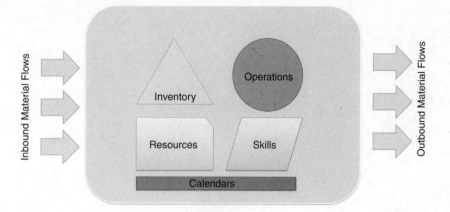

EXHIBIT 1.4 Anatomy of a Supply Chain Node

Inventory is consumed, produced, or distributed through these nodes. For example, inventory is consumed at the stores as customers buy the merchandise. Raw material is consumed at factories, and finished goods are produced in turn. A warehouse distributes the goods.

Operations are performed at these nodes. These operations can vary from manufacturing activities such as machining and assembly in a factory, to distribution activities such as receiving and shipping in a warehouse. Only certain types of operations can be performed at a certain location. For example, a pure cross-docking warehouse location may not stock inventory; therefore it can serve only those inbound shipments that are immediately used for fulfillment of outbound shipments. In another example, a factory may only have resources for machining operations while the final assembly of the product may be produced in a separate factory. This restricts the feasible paths for materials flowing through the supply chain network.

Resources are consumed by the operations at the node. However, resources have a limited capacity. For example, if it takes one hour to assemble a car on an assembly line, then you can produce only eight cars in an eight-hour workshift. This can constrain the flow of goods and services through that node in the network. This is called *throughput*. *Constraint-based planning* is one of the key differentiators of supply chain planning when compared to its predecessor MRP (master resource planning) processes, which assumed infinite materials and resources. We will cover this in more detail later.

Resources have *skills*, and therefore all resources may not be able to do all operations. For example, a receiving clerk in the warehouse may not be able to process shipments that require driving a forklift. This can further constrain the flow through a node. Enforcing these constraints during planning ensures that the plans produced by the supply chain processes are feasible as they guarantee the resource capacity as well as the right resources to be available for the operations and flows.

Consider a manufacturing example of an apparel-manufacturing factory. This location consumes fabric and thread, and produces shirts. These are all modeled as *inventory*. The *resources* at this *node* are people and machines used in producing these shirts. The *operation* at the node is the production of shirts. For the people to be productive at this location, they must have the *skills* for cutting and sewing the fabric for shirts. These last two parameters, and capacity of machines and operators together, will define the *throughput* at this node. Throughput is the rate of production or any other operation at a location. For example, the throughput or capacity of a shirt factory can be measured as the number of shirts produced every hour.

Now consider a retail example of a warehouse. Warehouses receive and may stock merchandise *inventory* for distribution to stores or customers. Warehouses have *operations* such as receiving and shipping. These operations need *resources* and *skills*. The warehouse is constrained by its storage capacity and resources available to receive and ship merchandise. There may be additional considerations at a warehouse, such as number of dock doors and trailers available, that affect the *throughput* of a warehouse node. The throughput of a warehouse can be measured as the number of inbound or outbound operations that it can handle in a day, or the volume of merchandise handled in a day in cases/packs/pallets or cubic feet.

Attributes of a Supply Chain Flow-path

The *flow-paths* connect the nodes in a supply chain. Together with the nodes, they create a supply chain network that represents the physical supply chain through which material, information, and resources flow. Exhibit 1.5 shows a supply chain flow-path and the typical elements modeled on a flow-path.

The flow-paths in a supply chain represent logical corridors between locations along which merchandise flows. They may represent physical routes and lanes or simply a logical model of these entities. What is important is that while *nodes* represent value addition through operations, the *flow-paths* simply represent *transfer* of material from one node to another without any other inherent value addition.

The *inventory* flows along the flow-paths but it is always in transit to or from a node. The *operation* on a flow-path is always transferring of material from one node to another.

However, flow-paths do constrain the flows and they can represent resources and skills, both of which together determine the capacity of a

EXHIBIT 1.5 Anatomy of a Supply Chain Flow-path

flow-path. The capacity here represents the available transfer/shipping capacity between the two locations. This capacity may be constrained due to carrier contracts in place or unavailability of the right type of equipment (flat-bed versus covered trailer), or simply availability of drivers on a route. Flow-paths also model the modes of transportation when required, such as road/rail/ocean and air.

An example of a flow-path is the route between a retailer's warehouse and the store. The trucks and trailers available on this route represent the *resources* on this flow-path. Ability to drive the trucks/trailers then represents the *skill* required to leverage the available resources. Together they determine the constraints along this flow-path and define the capacity available for transfer of merchandise between the two nodes.

Summary

Supply chain management consists of managing the flow of resources across the enterprise for efficient business operations. These resources can be people, materials, information, and other organizational assets such as vehicles and machinery.

Physical supply chains consist of factories, warehouses, stores, vendors, and other locations. These locations are modeled as nodes. Resources such as material and information can flow among these locations. These flows are modeled as flow-paths. The nodes and flow-paths model the real-life constraints that represent capacity and flow constraints along these paths. Together, these nodes and flow-paths allow modeling of the attributes and behavior of the physical supply chain networks. These models form the underlying concepts for understanding and resolving supply chain problems using technology solutions that increasingly use such modeling techniques, along with mathematical formulations to provide optimal and feasible solutions.

CHAPTER 2

Scope of the Supply Chain

A s with the definition, the scope of supply chains can vary widely. For the purpose of this discussion and to establish expectations, we would like to define the scope of the supply chain as follows: We see the supply chain as *core functions* and *extended functions*.

Core Supply Chain Functions

The core functions of the supply chain relate to activities that are limited to within the four walls of the corporation. These are the processes that are typically covered within what is called the *supply chain management (SCM) space*.

Examples of these functions are demand planning, supply planning, manufacturing, warehousing, transportation, supply chain visibility, and supply chain network optimization. These functions differ from those in the extended supply chain in that they are typically managed completely within the four walls of the corporations. While partner collaboration is desirable for these operations, it is not critical to their central intent. The data required for these functions is usually generated within the corporation and available without any constraints or privacy concerns. The changes to this data are governed by corporate policies and are therefore predictable.

While these functions generate data and transactions that can enable collaboration with partners, such partnering is typically beyond the scope of conventional SCM processes.

The core supply chain functions as described here remain the main focus of the current discussion. These processes will be discussed in detail, explained with examples, and constitute the heart of this book.

Extended Supply Chain Functions

The extended functions of the supply chain extend the processes at either end of the corporate supply chain, and create the extended supply chains representing the partners and enabling collaboration where relevant.

On the supply end, *supplier relationship management (SRM)* complements the SCM core processes. The SRM processes add the capability for bidding, bid analysis and awards, strategic sourcing, collaboration, supplier performance management, supplier compliance, and supplier score-carding. Most of the SRM processes are extremely relevant to the SCM discussion. While we may not go into as much detail on SRM functions, we will touch on these where relevant to provide the context.

On the demand end, *customer relationship management (CRM)* complements the SCM core processes. The CRM processes add the capability for quote and opportunity management, customer order and fulfillment management, returns and exchanges, customer collaboration, customer segmentation, profiling, and other customer analytics such as lifetime value and demographics, market-basket analysis, and so on. CRM processes may further support marketing functions like pricing, promotions, targeted marketing campaigns, and customer support functions through call centers. Different industries require different functions from the CRM landscape depending on their target customer, channels, type of merchandise, and maturity. CRM processes cover a large functional landscape and are largely beyond the scope of the current discussion, though we may briefly touch on them where relevant.

Exhibit 2.1 shows this relationship between the core and extended supply chain functions. The dotted line in this exhibit depicts the general scope of the supply chain functions that are covered in this book.

Supply Chain: Planning versus Execution

A few words on supply chain planning and execution are in order as the rest of the book is organized along these lines.

Supply chain planning typically consists of functions that produce a relatively longer-term picture for future operations. These processes are designed to provide decision-support tools for supply chain managers. They typically have a longer planning horizon, and are modeled at an abstract level and at a higher granularity than the physical assets of a supply chain. The planning processes provide the ability to create multiple scenarios and evaluate them for specific metrics to determine the optimal plans. They are generally modeled through complex mathematical models and solved for optimizing one of the overriding objectives. The

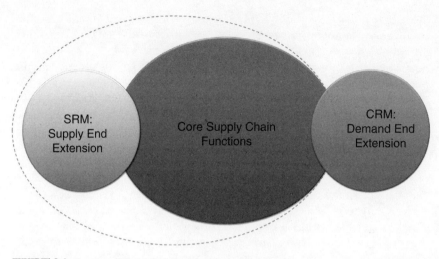

EXHIBIT 2.1 Core and Extended Supply Chain Functions

output of these planning processes is adopted by the execution processes for action.

One such process is inventory planning. This process typically determines inventory stocking levels, ordering frequency, and order quantities at all locations that need inventory. A typical inventory planning process is modeled at warehouse or store level, and needs demand and supply information in weekly or monthly buckets as the main input. Based on the user-defined target service level, this process can generate multiple scenarios for inventory deployment for minimizing inventory costs. Finally, the output of the inventory planning process is adopted as an input to the replenishment planning process that provides the purchase suggestions for execution.

Supply chain execution typically consists of functions for relatively short-term duration and for immediate execution of operations. These processes are designed to create an execution schedule for the target business function such as shipping to stores, or production schedules for a factory. They typically have a short execution horizon, and are modeled to closely reflect the physical assets of a supply chain. They may create multiple scenarios, though these scenarios are typically internal to the system for generating the best feasible solution. They can also leverage complex mathematical models or simple rules to create feasible execution schedules. Depending on the process, optimization may or may not be an overriding factor for execution processes. The output of these execution processes is activities that may create transactions for the host/ERP systems.

As an example of a supply chain execution process, let us consider inbound operations at a warehouse. These operations are typically planned for the next few days. They are planned based on the inbound purchase orders, or advance shipment notices (ASN). The output of the inbound planning process for a warehouse typically is the schedule of receiving and disposition activities for the warehouse. The process needs to model the warehouse assets to the lowest possible granularity, reflecting the physical assets like dock doors, forklifts, receiving associates, zones, aisles, and locations for creating a feasible execution schedule. The process in this example works fine with a set of decision rules to schedule receiving and for determining the disposition for the inbound inventory. Once executed, the process generates the inventory transactions that are sent to the host/ERP system.

A contrasting example of a supply chain execution process will be shipment planning for the inbound orders. This process also models all the relevant physical assets such as lanes, routes, transportation equipment, and modes, but typically leverages complex mathematical models to create the shipping plans. The overriding objective of this solution is to create a shipment plan that minimizes transportation cost and transports all the orders as required. The output of this process creates shipments that are executed by the carriers, suppliers, and receiving location (warehouse) associates. Once these shipments are executed, it may create carrier transactions for payments that are then integrated back into the resident host/ERP system for settlement.

Exhibit 2.2 shows an example of the planning and execution functions for a retail supply chain. At a high level, the retail supply chains cater to the three basic processes of buying, distributing the merchandise, and selling.

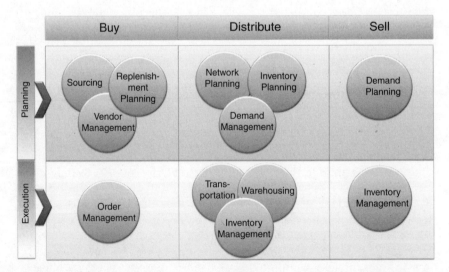

EXHIBIT 2.2 Examples of Retail Supply Chain Planning and Execution Functions

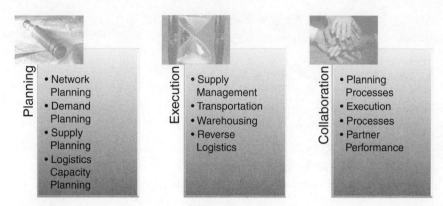

EXHIBIT 2.3 Overview of Supply Chain Landscape

Within the context of these high-level processes, the supply chain functions provide the capabilities for planning and execution. The exhibit shows that the buying process is supported by sourcing, replenishment planning, and vendor management functions in the planning tier, and by purchase order management in the execution tier. Together these functions will provide all core capabilities required to operate a retail supply chain's buying process.

Overview of the Supply Chain Landscape

Before heading off into individual functions, we present the overview of the supply chain landscape that is the subject of current discussion. Exhibit 2.3 shows the processes we will cover and how they are grouped. The discussions follow in the subsequent chapters.

The rest of this book is organized into the following parts, reflecting the organization of supply chain functions, also depicted in Exhibit 2.3.

Part Two: Supply Chain Planning

In this part, we will cover the decision-support processes that help in longer-term planning and forecasting, and help the users evaluate various possible scenarios and pick the most optimal for execution. The network planning, demand planning, supply planning, and logistics planning processes will be covered within this part of the text. Exhibit 2.4 shows an overview of the supply chain planning functions.

These are the processes that are generally used as a decision-support system rather than for supporting immediate execution. The output of these processes typically gets adopted by the execution functions as input

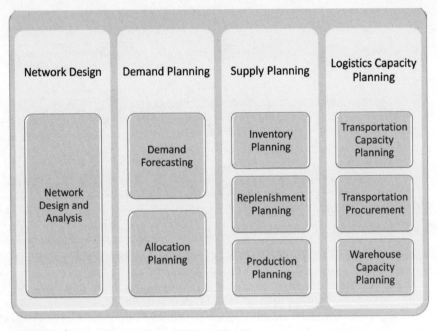

EXHIBIT 2.4 Supply Chain Planning Functions

decision parameters. For example, the projected replenishment needs computed by the replenishment planning process will drive the purchase orders created and managed as part of the replenishment execution functions. This relationship allows the operations of an enterprise to be aligned with its plans, making sure that the immediate actions help achieve the longer-term objectives of the organization.

The network planning processes help in establishing the network of nodes and flow-paths that models the physical supply chain for optimal cost or flow performance. Demand planning processes help in determining the projected demand that the enterprise should plan to address. Supply planning identifies the sources of supply to address the identified demand and establishes how this demand will be fulfilled, either through purchases or manufacturing. Logistics planning processes look at the projected logistics capacity requirements to support the demand and supply projections, and help the organization evaluate the existing routes and facilities and their capacities.

Most of the planning processes require a clear business strategy, clean historical data, and a good understanding of the modeling and solution constraints. As these processes generally do not have an immediate impact but help in aligning the operations with the long-term goals of the corporation, they may appear to have a low effort-to-value ratio. However,

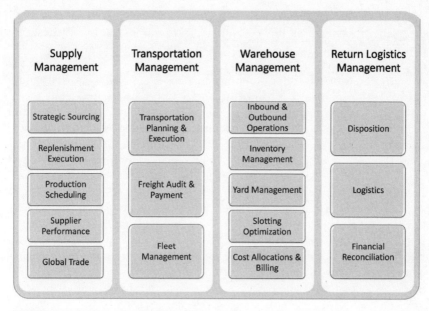

Supply Management	Transportation Management	Warehouse Management	Return Logistics Management
Strategic Sourcing	Transportation Planning & Execution	Inbound & Outbound Operations	Disposition
Replenishment Execution		Inventory Management	
Production Scheduling	Freight Audit & Payment	Yard Management	Logistics
Supplier Performance		Slotting Optimization	
Global Trade	Fleet Management	Cost Allocations & Billing	Financial Reconciliation

EXHIBIT 2.5 Supply Chain Execution Functions

underestimating their value in providing cost and operational efficiencies is a mistake.

Part Three: Supply Chain Execution

This part covers the processes that help run the day-to-day operations. These processes typically take the outputs or decision parameters from the planning processes and operate within the constraints provided by the planning parameters. Supply management (ordering, manufacturing), transportation, warehousing, and reverse logistics execution fall into this section. Exhibit 2.5 shows an overview of these functions.

The supply management functions help in procurement of material and capacity that will be required to fulfill the immediate demand. For a retailer, this may be the management of merchandise purchase orders, while for a manufacturer this may consist of procuring the raw materials and establishing a production planning schedule that allows the manufacturer to fill the demand. Transportation and warehousing functions help in management of flow and stocking of materials required to keep the business running smoothly. These two functions are very critical to a retailer's total supply chain costs, and are important for retailers as well as manufacturers to run their operations smoothly. Reverse logistics functions provide the ability to return merchandise to vendors, such returns being the result of customer returns, bad quality, vendor buybacks, and other similar reasons.

The vendor-facing functions of sourcing and purchasing straddle both the planning as well as the execution processes; in this book, these are covered together under the supply chain execution functions for an easy, continuous discussion of the subject.

Supply chain execution supports the processes that help in running day-to-day operations of a company. These processes are frequently based on the results of the supply chain planning processes. Such adoption from a planning process is highly desirable. It has two distinct benefits: It ensures that the supply chain operations are aligned with the plans, and it guarantees a feasible plan of execution if the higher-level planning was conducted with properly modeled constraints. As a result, the operational plans can be executed with minimal changes.

The focus of the supply chain execution functions is immediate; they create transactions as they execute the plans, and help in managing the operations smoothly. The output from the supply chain execution processes is very often integrated into the resident enterprise resource planning (ERP) system of a company as these transactions affect inventory, financials, and other aspects that the ERP systems need to know about.

In fact, the supply chain planning and execution processes need to be tightly integrated with each other as well as with the resident ERP systems. The supply chain planning processes typically need the transaction histories, budgets, and financial plan data from the ERP system to establish the decision parameters. The supply chain execution functions adopt these decision parameters and help carry out the operations. These operations generate transactions that become part of ERP transaction lifecycles. This relationship between the supply chain functions and the ERP systems is shown in Exhibit 2.6.

Throughout the discussion on supply chain execution functions, such interdependency of supply chain execution and ERP systems has been indicated. In fact, the integration between these two systems is almost always a big concern for the companies evaluating these solutions, and can substantially affect the deployment effort and timelines.

Part Four: Supply Chain Collaboration

The section on supply chain collaboration covers the supply chain processes that can be best achieved through collaboration with the partners. Collaboration is not a prerequisite for these processes, but can create huge process efficiencies if available. Examples of such processes are demand collaboration and supply collaboration. Active demand collaboration with the suppliers allows the whole supply chain to react quickly to any demand changes and maximize its ability to optimally fulfill this demand.

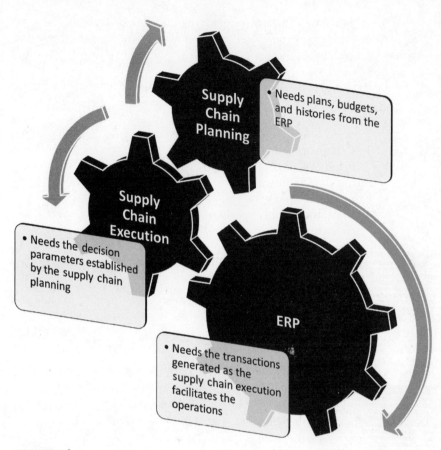

EXHIBIT 2.6 Supply Chain Functions and ERP Systems

This section also leverages the distinction between the planning and execution processes by identifying those processes where active collaboration is most useful. Partner performance measurement is also covered under the supply chain collaboration process.

Summary

The scope of supply chains extends through the organization from the demand end to the supply end. However, the core supply chain functions primarily relate to the demand and supply management processes directly controlled by the enterprise. CRM extends the demand end of supply chains and provides processes for influencing demand by managing customers, prices, and marketing strategies. On the supply end, SRM processes extend the supply chains by managing sourcing and suppliers to ensure reliable sources for fulfilling the demand.

The core supply chain functions themselves can be viewed as planning functions or execution functions. The planning functions project a longer-term view of enterprise plans, allow what-if analysis, and provide the impact of these plans on corporate financial/operational metrics. These planning processes primarily serve as decision-support tools for managers. Examples of the supply chain planning functions are network planning, demand planning, and supply planning. The execution functions provide the schedule of daily operations, and help the enterprise execute the selected supply chain plans through purchasing, manufacturing, distributing, and sales operations. Examples of the supply chain execution functions are transportation and warehousing operations.

Finally, supply chain collaboration processes enable sharing the planning and execution process data with the supply chain partners with the intention of enhancing the responsiveness and flexibility of the supply chain. Examples of collaborative processes are demand and supply collaboration with the suppliers or carrier portal to monitor and track shipments.

PART II

Supply Chain Planning

CHAPTER 3

Supply Chain Network Design

Supply chain network design is the process of establishing the network *nodes* and *flow-paths* in a supply chain. These nodes can represent either of manufacturing, stocking, or distribution locations. This process helps plan the most desirable physical locations and their types that will constitute the supply chain for most efficient flow of materials and merchandise. The selling locations (such as stores) are outside the scope of this process as the factors governing the ideal location of a store are very different from those of warehouses or manufacturing plants.

Supply chain network design is a critical process for distribution-intensive industries such as retail. In such industries, the cost of distribution of merchandise is a substantial part of their total operational costs. Large retailers typically have thousands of stores and may have hundreds of warehouses. Together, this network creates a complex set of flow-paths along which the merchandise can flow. An optimally designed network can substantially reduce the costs and lead-time for distribution. This is also true for large manufacturers that have vendors, factories, and warehouses distributed across geographies and can benefit from optimizing their network flows.

Some of the questions that this process answers are:

- What is the best network configuration to address the current and projected demand patterns while maintaining desired service and cost levels? How many facilities are required, and where should they be? What does it mean in terms of inventory deployment?
- Do the warehouses have enough capacity for the current and future operations? Can they handle optimal product flows within the warehouse for all types of products (conveyable/nonconveyable)?
- Which stores will be replenished from each warehouse?
- What transport modes and lanes are best to move products through the network? Is there enough negotiated capacity along each flow-path in the network?

- What is the cost of maintaining and operating the current network? How is this cost affected by various scenarios where certain facilities are closed, expanded, or contracted, or new ones started?

In most cases, this network of suppliers, warehouses, and stores is a combination of organic growth and deliberate planning. When the companies are small, their supply chains are simple and easier to manage. As the companies grow, so do their supply chains. They become complex and expensive to manage. Planning and managing them effectively becomes a clear differentiator.

Optimal supply chain network design helps in controlling the capital as well as operational costs. For retailers, the cost of distribution is the second largest cost after the direct cost of merchandise. The retail store locations are determined based on customer demographics and competition, and are largely independent of supply chain operation cost considerations. But other locations, such as those required for warehousing or manufacturing, can be planned based on supply chain operational costs. The choice of these locations and type of operations they support impacts the fixed costs of land, buildings, and equipment, as well as the variable costs of personnel, utilities, transportation, maintenance, and so on.

The objective of the supply chain network design process is to minimize these operational costs, while maintaining the ability of the supply chain to effectively service the demand and supply requirements. This function allows the business to model the existing supply chain operations, with the planned supply chain growth, and evaluate the operating costs of the network for each option.

Inputs and Outputs of the Supply Chain Network Design Process

This process considers the following inputs:

- Existing locations of stores (also called *consuming* locations). For the new Web-based businesses, without any physical stores, the equivalent inputs will be the number of individual orders fulfilled in specific regions. For manufacturers, this will be the receiving locations of their customers' warehouses.
- Existing and/or proposed locations of warehouses or factories (also called *supplying* locations). This may also include the locations of the shipping warehouses for the major vendors.
- Products carried at each of the locations (warehouses and stores).
- Fixed- and variable-cost models for each of the locations for stocking, handling, shipping, and other warehouse activities.

- Cost models for transportation lanes/routes (also called *flow-paths*) between the above nodes and transportation modes.
- Volume of goods transported along these flow-paths based on historical data, and future projections for the same, as well as desired inventory/service levels at the receiving nodes.
- Other costs are modeled that reflect the cost of opening a new facility or closing an existing facility. These costs may also be weighted by the user to reflect the user bias toward closing existing facilities or opening new facilities.

The process then consists of either computing the cost of the existing network model to operate or suggesting new locations or changes to existing locations in the network.

The solutions supporting the network planning process routinely utilize mathematical programming to formulate and solve the problem for minimizing the total costs of operating the network.

The output of the process may consist of the following:

- Multiple scenarios with different locations and costs of running the network in each scenario
- Proposed new locations and their size, or changes to existing locations including expanding, contracting, or closing the existing facilities
- Projected product volumes at nodes and flow-paths

Applications supporting the network planning process provide rich user workflows for creating, evaluating, and comparing alternative scenarios. They also provide visualization tools for pictorial representations of the supply chain network typically superimposed on a map to provide geographic context.

The actual selection and building of a facility requires further study around the proposed locations and will consider additional inputs such as labor market, demographics, education levels, and so on. However, the optimization process helps in narrowing down such choices and helps direct these efforts on a sound cost-based initial analysis.

Due to high-level of capital investments and the long lead times involved in setting up the distribution centers, the supply chain network process covers a longer-term horizon. This is truly a decision-support system to help the users make objective decisions based on cost analysis.

The output of the process is widely adopted by most of the supply chain processes that need the supply chain network model. Demand and supply planning applications use the network models to propagate the demand and supplies across the network echelons to create location-specific plans.

Related Subprocesses

These subprocesses enhance and extend the scope of the supply chain network planning process. The product flow-path analysis generally concerns itself with the flow of merchandise within a specific physical facility. The logistics capacity planning is simply a byproduct of the network planning and provides the basis for carrier capacity and warehouse capacities required to support the selected network.

Product Flow Analysis in the Warehouse

The objective of this process is to optimize the product flowing through a warehouse. This may mean reducing the cost of handling within the warehouse, reducing the time between receiving the inventory and determining its disposition, or automating the handling where possible.

When merchandise is received in a warehouse, it can be put away for future shipments to stores, cross-docked for immediate shipment, conveyed to the staging location, put away to an assembly area, and so on. In all cases, several more options exist.

For example, if it is to be put away, it can be stored in the *reserve locations* or *active pick locations*. Reserve locations generally provide mass storage, and putting away the merchandise in the reserve locations typically provides the stock for future fulfillment of orders. Active pick locations are closer to the shipping docks, more accessible to pickers, and can improve the order-fulfillment operations considerably. Merchandise in the active pick locations is replenished from the reserve locations.

Similarly, cross-docking can be preplanned or opportunistic. Preplanned cross-docking is based on the planned inbound shipments at the warehouse and planned order shipments outbound to the stores. This cross-docking activity is part of the warehouse planning and is typically completed a few days in advance. Opportunistic cross-docking is an instantaneous decision by the system to match an inbound shipment with an outbound order to create a cross-docking task. Cross-docking may also involve breaking pallets when the outbound orders are smaller, and warehouses are allowed to ship cases/boxes or eaches.

Conveyable and nonconveyable merchandise in the warehouses also takes different physical paths and may have different disposition rules. *Conveyable merchandise* lends itself to automated flow through the warehouse, and therefore will have limited options based on the available mechanization. *Nonconveyable merchandise* typically requires manual handling but also provides greater flexibility for disposition decisions. However, warehouse productivity can be greatly enhanced through automating where possible and by reducing the human touchpoints in the process.

The product flow analysis helps the planners to decide what would be the best disposition of the incoming inventory in the warehouse, and the best way to execute that disposition. For example, when boxes prelabeled for shipping to stores are received, it may be most cost efficient to convey them directly from the receiving dock to the staging area using automated conveyors and bar-code readers that can direct them to their destined staging area. This will reduce the manual touchpoints, as well as the cost of labor in handling these boxes. However, this can be achieved only when the merchandise is received in conveyable boxes, and labels are formatted to a certain standard with high rate of compliance. Not all merchandise will fall in this category. Nonconveyable merchandise, such as furniture, must be carried using forklifts, but touchpoints can be reduced by cross-docking such merchandise or by selecting appropriate stocking locations. The handling requirements for the merchandise in the warehouse will also change from season to season as the product demand ramps up or down. The product flow analysis process can help in determining the relevant factors affecting the disposition and stocking in the warehouse, and therefore in reducing the total handling costs.

The *inbound merchandise flow disposition* in the warehouse is determined based on several inventory and demand characteristics. The optimal choice depends on a number of factors, including product dimensions (conveyable or nonconveyable), seasonality characteristics (in-season or out-of-season), sales pattern (slow moving or fast moving), inventory levels, and other factors such as new products or promotions. Considering these factors, the planners determine the best flow-path for a season. The merchandise then follows that standard flow-path within the warehouse until these paths are reviewed and changed. The frequency of this review may coincide with product seasonality, new product introductions, clearances, promotion and holiday ramp-ups, and inventory policy changes.

Using historical and projected product demand and supply patterns, inventory attributes, product attributes, and warehouse characteristics for analysis can help in determining the best flow of products within the warehouse. These recommendations evolve and change with variations in assortments, time, and inventory plans.

Logistics Capacity Planning

Future capacity planning for logistics (warehousing and transportation) operations is another process related to network planning. Based on the projected sales plans, the network planning process can help in projecting warehousing and transportation capacity needs over the years. Analyzing these requirements can help in better planning for a growing network. Such plans may require changing warehousing capacity by opening new warehouses, expanding existing ones, mechanizing warehouses to increase throughput, and negotiating transportation contracts in advance to address the projected changes for the transportation capacity.

As opening a new warehouse can take a long time, the projected growth in logistics capacity requirements provides useful information for planning and action in advance.

Summary

Supply chain network processes help in evaluating the manufacturing, distribution, supply, and sales networks. As companies grow, supply chain efficiencies are impacted due to the changes in demand and supply patterns. The network planning functions provide methods for evaluating the current networks and determining the optimal design for future networks using the forecasted or planned demand and supply projections.

Network design and optimization for supply chains allows corporations to plan their growth to be aligned with their business strategy, growth targets, and projected changes in demand for their products. As making any changes in the network is capital intensive and takes time to implement, network evaluation and optimization remains a decision-support process that should be part of a business planning exercise and should be conducted at least annually.

The process also allows corporations to effectively manage their growth in logistics requirements by accurately projecting warehousing and transportation needs.

CHAPTER 4

Demand Planning

The objective of the demand planning process is to forecast the demand for products so that this demand can be fulfilled through existing inventory, manufacturing, and new purchases. Demand planning is done for a product at a location for a given time bucket. Demand planning is probably the most important supply chain process in that it drives almost all other processes directly or indirectly toward fulfilling the demand.

The projected demand determines what a retailer should buy or a manufacturer should build. This in turn drives the factory capacity and resource utilization, raw material demand, and orders on vendors for such raw material.

Within the enterprise, the demand is projected at the downstream or demand end of the supply chain and gets propagated through the network until it is satisfied with the supply from a supplying node. For example, demand at a store will be propagated to the upstream warehouse. If the warehouse can satisfy this demand from the available inventory, then the demand propagation stops at this node. If the warehouse does not have enough available inventories, then the rest of the demand signal will be propagated to the next upstream node in the supply chain, which can be a vendor or another warehouse.

The supply chain within an enterprise can be considered simply a part of the larger supply chain consisting of supply chains of many such enterprises. Extending this example, when the warehouse is unable to satisfy the store demand, it must place an order on its vendor. Through this order the demand is conveyed to the vendor's supply chain, which in turn must start propagating the demand signal upstream until it can be addressed.

Demand planning consists of various subprocesses:

- *Demand forecasting* provides the projected forecast into the future usually based on the historical data for the specified product-location combination.

■ *Allocation planning*, also sometimes called *push-based replenishment*, is the part of the demand management process that allows for managing seasonal merchandise in an effective manner.

■ *Replenishment planning* takes the unconstrained demand forecasts as input and generates the replenishment plan, taking the available inventory into consideration.

Together these processes answer the following questions:

■ What is the unconstrained projected (forecast) demand for a product at a location at a specific time?

■ What do I need to fulfill this demand? How much inventory do I need at various points in the network to ensure that the demand at all consuming nodes can be fulfilled?

Demand Forecasting

Demand forecasting is the process of using the sales history of a product at a location and projecting the demand into the future. Most of the forecasting solutions use statistical methods for projecting the future demand. Such statistical methods can vary from a simple moving average, to curve-fitting techniques, to time series analysis.

Demand forecasting simply answers the question, "What is the projected demand forecast for a product at a location at a specific time based on the historical sales of that product at that location?" This process provides the input for all the subsequent processes for demand planning.

It is important to determine the level at which the demand should be forecasted. Retailers routinely forecast demand for what they sell, while manufacturers may forecast demand for subassemblies rather than the finished goods. For example, consider a computer manufacturer. It is almost impossible to precisely determine the demand in a given time period of a laptop computer with a 2 GHz dual processor, 2 GB RAM, and 250 GB HDD. However, if the demand is forecast for the subassemblies, such as the motherboard, RAM module, HDD, and so on, then a more accurate and reliable forecast can be produced. The manufacturing schedule can be planned using the subassembly demand while the final assembly can be finished quickly after the order is received.

Forecasts can be used for various processes in an enterprise. For example, forecasts can be used for replenishment or for price optimization. Longer-term revenue forecasts can also be used for business strategy development, business planning/budgeting, infrastructure planning, and other long-term investments. A single product forecast that can be used for all the enterprise processes would produce decisions that are fully aligned with the planned changes in demand. However, these processes may need to consolidate the projected demand at differing levels of data granularity, and in different units, namely, dollars or quantity. Therefore, a single forecast solution should allow for manipulating the forecasts such that they can be consolidated along organizational hierarchies, product families, regional hierarchies, and time. It also requires that forecasts can be viewed either as number of units or as dollars.

For example, demand forecasts used by a manufacturer to decide on capital investments required for factories will most likely be consolidated and viewed at a product-family level that requires similar production facilities on an annual basis. This will help in establishing the future manufacturing capacity requirements so that forecasted capacities can be compared with existing infrastructure to drive capital investments. Chances are that investment dollars will be prioritized toward product families that are more profitable than others, or have a stable demand over long periods of time.

However, a demand forecast produced to drive the replenishment and ordering process will be at the lowest product-location level for the immediate days/weeks. This forecast will be in sales units as it is expected to drive the inventories and ordering quantities.

Demand forecasting extensively uses historical sales data. However, there are various other factors that affect demand. These factors must be analyzed and considered in the demand forecasting algorithms. Examples of some of the factors that affect demand are prices, seasons, new products, promotions, and even weather. Most of the demand forecasting solutions available these days provide modeling to accommodate these factors. However, this may frequently require understanding the sales history to analyze the historical impact of such factors on demand to model the projected impact in the future. A great amount of data analysis is usually part of any demand forecasting solution deployment for a successful outcome.

Here are some terms related to the process of demand forecasting that are useful to know:

Seasonality is the nature of demand when the demand shows a repeating (seasonal) pattern over time. Products that are identified to have seasonal demand can use special forecasting methods for optimal results.

Seasonal indices is a list of index numbers that build the seasonal profile. For example, if a season lasts six weeks, and demand during the six weeks rises to 1.1 times the average normal demand in week 1, then to 1.3 in week 2 until it reaches 1.6 times in week 4, to drop to 1.1 in week 5, and to average in week 6, then the factors in this example will constitute the seasonal indices for the specific product/location. A seasonal demand pattern is sometimes *de-seasonalized* using these indices, leaving behind an average demand line that is more stable and can be used for forecasting more easily. The indices are put back on the forecasted demand to recreate the seasonal effect.

Price elasticity of demand refers to the relationship between the price and demand of an item. Usually the demand rises if the price drops, and vice versa. However, for items such as gas, the price may not have any significant impact on the demand, and such demand is assumed to be inelastic. However, for most products the price elasticity is real, and demand planning solutions use the historical price with the historical demand to establish this correlation and use it for projecting future demand.

Promotions and other events can affect demand. Promotions typically take advantage of the price elasticity of demand, and are planned events. The planned events can be analyzed for their impact on demand to adjust the historical data to accurately reflect true demand. However, unplanned events such as weather can affect the demand as well, and it may be harder to isolate the impact of such unplanned events on the historical demand data.

Data spike or *demand spike* is said to occur when the demand in a specific time bucket exceeds the average demand by a large amount. Normally a deviation of 2 or 3 σ (denoting *standard deviation*) from the average is considered a spike. As spikes can destabilize a time series, users can configure the system to ignore the spike, replace it with a predefined outer limit on deviation, or change it to series average.

Data cleansing is the process of cleaning suspect sales data prior to using it for forecasting. Suspect data can be systematically flagged using rules, and can be sometimes resolved algorithmically or through user intervention.

Lost sales is the correction applied to the sales history data to account for lost sales. When a customer walks in the store but does not find what he needs, that is a lost sale. Even though this data will not be captured in the sales history, it is relevant to compute the forecast demand as it reflects the true sales if that product were never out of stock. Standard lost-sales algorithms can capture and compensate for this. Forecasting solutions may have such features as standard.

Causal factors are factors that compensate for the impact on sales due to an external event. These factors model the events that affect sales. These may be planned events such as promotions, or unplanned events such as a cold front. The intent of identifying and applying causal factors is to normalize the sales history to reflect the effect of these events. Sales history can be analyzed to identify causal factors and to define the effect of these events. The same model factor can then be applied to the forecasted demand to reproduce the effect of a planned event that is similar to the historical event.

Curve fitting is a statistical technique of converting a list of numbers (such as sales history data) to a mathematical equation. This equation is then used for future projections. The curve-fitting process finds a curve that has the best fit for the given series of data points. It may also be called *interpolation*, or sometimes *regression analysis*.

Time series is a sequence of data points measured at successive and generally uniform time intervals. *Sales history* is a time series as it measures sales on a timescale (e.g., daily, weekly, etc.). *Time series analysis* is the collective name for methods that are used to explain such time series, and to forecast the series into the future.

Trend may exist in any time series when the time series graph shows a consistent upward or downward trend in numbers over time. Trends may forecast a growth or decline in the product sales. Upward or downward trends must extend over a large period of time to be significant. Forecast moving up for two forecast periods may not signify a trend, but a consistent upward or downward movement over a few months or a year may well be a trend.

Best pick is a method deployed by several forecasting techniques that consists of creating multiple forecasts for a single time series, computing the forecast error for all of the results, and then picking up the best result (with the smallest forecast errors) for persistence.

Inputs and Outputs of the Demand Forecasting Process

Demand forecasting process needs the following inputs:

- Master data such as items/products, locations, planning horizon, and valid item-location combinations. The item-location combination is also called *assortment,* especially when used in the context of a store.
- Sales or consumption history along with the price history at each of the valid product-location combinations.
- User and system configurations such as inputs for forecasting algorithms, classification of products as slow/fast movers, seasonality identifiers, causal factors that may have affected history, data cleansing parameters, and so on. Each of these input factors may direct the behavior of the solution.

The demand forecasting process then uses the sales history, price history, events, and seasonal factors, and determines the optimal statistical algorithm for generating the forecast for the selected planning horizon. Some of the available solutions will also generate the forecast errors, tracking signals, and other process metrics during the process.

The output of the process consists of the following:

- The projected unconstrained forecast for all product-location combinations for the selected planning horizon
- Forecasting process metrics such as forecast errors, tracking signals, and so on

Related Subprocesses

The demand forecasting process heavily depends on the data. This data changes frequently, and can have extremely large volumes if collected at the store-product-day level. Another equally important data stream for a well-functioning demand forecasting system is causal factors. The following subprocesses help ensure such data quality dependencies of the process.

CAUSAL FACTOR MANAGEMENT   Causal factors model any planned or unplanned events that can impact sales. It is important to understand and separately identify the effects of such events for better forecasts.

Examples of planned events are marketing campaigns, promotions, and clearance events. These events are easier to track, their dates are precisely known, and therefore they can be easily cross-referenced with the sales history data to identify the impact due to such planned events. The data for such events generally comes from the promotion management applications. This data is extracted and cross-referenced with the sales history using effective event dates to study the effect of the event on sales.

Unplanned events can also impact sales. Examples of such events are weather events and early or late seasons. These events need to be tracked separately so that their impact on the sales is known. Most retailers are currently unable to track weather events and their effects in a systematic fashion.

Other events that may be tied to holiday seasons, national sporting events, and so on, can also affect sales. Holidays can change dates from year to year, and therefore analysis of the effect of holiday sales from last year on projected sales may need to be adjusted on time axis.

Causal factor management processes can address all of these issues. These processes are quite often supported within the demand forecasting solutions. The data for planned events is generally available from the marketing systems that plan promotions and other events. Holiday and seasonal data may be required to be maintained manually (remember that the season dates may change from one region to another and from one year to the next). The weather data is hardest to obtain and use, though specialized demand forecasting applications that allow factoring in the effects of weather are now available.

DEMAND FORECASTING PROCESS ANALYTICS The demand forecasting process uses statistical methods for projecting historical data into the future. The process selects the best possible method for forecasting future demand based on various user and system inputs. Statistical parameters are also provided by the users to account for various types of demand characteristics, such as lumpy demand, seasonal demand, and so on.

Over time, demand patterns change and it is important to continuously tune the system to produce optimal forecasts. Forecast errors and tracking signals are computed by the system for this purpose. Forecast errors measure the difference between forecast and actual values of demand. There are various measures for forecast errors, such as *mean absolute deviation (MAD), mean absolute percent deviation or error (MAPD or MAPE), cumulative forecast error,* and *mean forecast error.* The forecast errors measure historical accuracy of the forecasts and are reactive in nature.

Tracking signals or *bias* can be used to predict when the forecasts are about to start trending up or down consistently compared to actual sales. This helps the users to tune the parameters to bring the forecasts closer to actual and reduce forecasting errors. A tracking signal is calculated as the cumulative error divided by MAD. The tracking signal basically shows the trend in the forecast error itself, and helps users pinpoint when a forecast model needs adjustments.

Trend reports and planned-versus-actual reports can also be very useful, even though these normally provide after-the-fact analysis of the situation.

Waterfall or cascade analysis is another tool that can be used for analyzing the health of the process. Waterfall analysis compares the forecasts produced in weeks N, $N + 1$, $N + 2$, and so on for a specific target time bucket, and compares these to actual sales. For example, you may take the actual sales from the current week and compare this with the forecast sales for this week that was produced four weeks prior, three weeks prior, two weeks prior, and last week. You should expect that the forecast produced last week was the most accurate compared to the forecasts produced two or three weeks in advance. Normally, the forecast becomes more accurate as the target time bucket approaches. Any other results may indicate tuning issues.

CONSENSUS FORECAST Demand forecast can be used as an input to a number of planning processes in an organization. For example, in retail environments, demand forecast can be used to determine required purchases, optimal pricing, supplies from warehouses to stores, sourcing, warehouse and transportation capacities, planogramming, and so on. In manufacturing, the demand forecasts may drive the production planning and scheduling, raw-material purchases, assembly capacities, and distribution schedules. Therefore, having a single forecast to consistently drive these planning processes has its advantages. Such a forecast is called a *consensus forecast*.

Statistical forecasts can be reviewed and enriched further with user inputs and a consensus forecast can be created that can be used as input to various other planning functions. The process of creating a consensus forecast primarily consists of bringing together the supply and demand groups and reviewing the forecasts, making changes, and agreeing to a single forecast.

In most organizations, sales teams own the demand forecasts, and the replenishment teams (consisting of merchants or inventory planners in retail, and manufacturing teams in manufacturing sectors) own the supplies. Creating a consensus forecast that both of these groups can agree to results in smoother operations for all, with a predictable and planned fulfillment rate for the demand.

The consensus forecast process is sometimes also called *sales and operations planning* and may be an extended exercise where demand as well as supply numbers are collaboratively agreed on by the different groups involved in the exercise. Sales and operations planning is most relevant in manufacturing industries as the process helps in aligning the forecasted demand with the manufacturing operations, making sure that the projected demand from the sales teams is actually acknowledged and planned for production by the manufacturing teams.

Either way, the objective of the process is to create a single forecast that the whole organization can work with.

Allocation Planning

Preorder allocation planning is another strategy for replenishments. The forecasting-based replenishment described in the previous section is generally suitable for a large number of items that have consistent demand, predictable seasonal demand, or cyclical demand that can be modeled using statistics. This type of replenishment strategy is sometimes called *pull-based* strategy. This is because the replenishment at any given node is based on the demand signals from the downstream node that *pulls* the merchandise from the target node. Consider a store that requests merchandise from the warehouse when needed. This is an example of pull-based replenishment, where the store pulls the merchandise from the warehouse as the need arises.

In contrast, there are situations where a merchant may simply choose to plan for demand in a different fashion. This is called a *push-based* replenishment strategy as it generally involves a merchant's decision to *push* merchandise to the stores without the stores explicitly asking for it. Examples of situations where this strategy will work best are one-time buys, unique holiday assortments, unique seasonal assortments, special deals with the suppliers, and so on.

Most retailers will have both replenishment strategies to cover planning for their complete assortment. Like the replenishment planning, the objective of the preorder allocation planning process is to generate the demand numbers for various products at relevant locations for the planning horizon. The primary difference is that these numbers are generally based on a merchant's experience and his or her interpretation of historical data, and not mathematically computed as in the case of the forecast-based replenishment plans.

Allocation planning processes answer the following questions:

- What is the target sales plan for a product category, and how does the merchant or the product manager plan to achieve that sales target? How is that sales target allocated across locations and products?
- How much inventory is needed at various points in the network to ensure that the demand at all nodes can be fulfilled to achieve the planned sales targets?

Inputs and Outputs of the Allocation Planning Process

The allocation planning process needs the following inputs:

- Master data such as items/products, locations, planning horizon, and valid item-location combinations. The item-location combination is also called *assortment,* especially when used in the context of a store. In addition, allocation needs the products and locations identified that will be replenished using this push-based replenishment process.
- Historical analysis for the selected products and locations. If no history is available, the merchant may use the average history of products in the category to which the specific products belong. It is also usual practice to use averages across similar products, store clusters, and so on to understand the historical demand that becomes the basis for the allocation planning. In addition to the historical sales data, merchants may also use planned sales data for these categories.
- User inputs for the inventories to be allocated, rules, indices, and strategies to compute the allocation numbers for the selected set of products and locations. These rules may distribute the inventory in equal parts,

in user-defined percentages, or use historical data to split the available inventory into allocations proportional to the sales in the selected history.

- On-hand inventory and expected receipts and shipments of inventory.
- Inventory policies, for example, the safety stock/cover required to be maintained, frequency of replenishment, replenishment quantities, and replenishment levels.
- Inventory flow constraints between the nodes (e.g., minimum, maximum, multiples) that must be met.

The process then produces the allocation numbers for each node and rounds them off to comply with the inventory flow parameters between the supplying and receiving node. It provides the following output:

- Allocated replenishment quantities at the nodes for the allocated products for each time period defined for the plan horizon.

Related Subprocesses

Allocation planning generally requires good historical data, tools for data analysis, and visual presentation so that the merchants can clearly understand the implications of their decisions. The solutions for supporting these processes should support simulations and alternative scenario evaluations to understand the costs of inventory, service-level impact, projected sales and profitability, and plan (open-to-buy) analysis. These processes then help the user to make good decisions for the new purchases, and for allocating the committed buys that are in the pipeline.

OPEN-TO-BUY   *Open-to-buy* refers to the process of reviewing seasonal purchases and comparing them with actual sales, projected sales at the onset of the season, planned sales for the rest of the season, on-hand inventories, and inventory on order either committed or open. This provides the planners a chance to change the open orders if the actual sales do not reflect the seasonal forecasts closely. For example, if the actual rate of sales is substantially lower than the projections for the season, this process will allow the planners to reduce the order quantities of the affected products and avoid having fresh inventory delivered that must then be cleared on discount. Alternatively, if sales pick up unexpectedly during the initial part of the season, planners can expedite the orders to ramp up inventories quickly to meet the rising demand.

The open-to-buy planning concept is widely used in the retail industry to manage seasonal merchandise.

Summary

Demand planning processes provide the tools for understanding, projecting, and managing demand in the supply chain network. The demand end of the supply chain normally generates the independent demand for products. This demand can be forecasted using various statistical techniques, some of which allow modeling of various factors that may affect demand, such as seasonality, weather zones, prices, and promotions. This forecasted demand is then propagated through the supply chain network to generate the demand plans at each of the supply chain nodes. These plans help the organization to manage the flow of materials, and create replenishment plans for supplies from internal and external sources.

A pull-based supply chain system anticipates the demand at the downstream end of the supply chain, and propagates the demand signal throughout the network to produce demand plans at every node of the chain. Pull-based systems generally use the replenishment planning processes to create supply plans.

A push-based supply chain plans for the supplies at the upstream end and propagates these planned supplies through the network in response to anticipated demand. Push-based systems typically use the allocation planning processes to create supply plans, and cater to seasonal goods. Open-to-buy processes support the allocation planning functions by providing periodic review of the demand and supply, allowing the managers to change the future supplies to align with the changing demand during the season.

Both of these systems can be simultaneously used for different categories of products, and for different manufacturing models to support an efficient supply chain.

CHAPTER 5

Supply Planning

The supply planning processes complement the demand planning functions in a supply chain. Once the net demand has been calculated, the next step is to create the supply plan to fulfill the demand. All the functions that help in the fulfillment of demand are collectively covered under the supply planning processes. These processes primarily cover inventory planning, purchase planning, production planning, and supply (or order) allocation functions. The supply planning functions are further supplemented by execution functions such as sourcing, production scheduling, purchase order management, and vendor management functions, which are discussed under the supply chain execution processes. These functions together help fulfill the planned demand.

Inventory Planning

The inventory planning process establishes the optimal inventory levels that must be maintained to meet expected fulfillment service levels. Any two nodes in a supply chain can be viewed as having a supplier–consumer relationship as the material flows from one node to another. When viewed as such, the node that acts as a consumer is placing demand on the node that acts as a supplier. This demand must be fulfilled by the supplying node at a user-specified fulfillment service level. To guarantee such service levels, the supplying node must maintain an optimal level of inventory. Artificially high service levels will push these inventory levels too high, and result in unusually high inventory costs and low inventory turns. The relationship between the amount of inventory required and service level is exponential, and therefore every little improvement in service levels will push the inventory levels higher and higher.

The following terms are useful to know in the context of inventory planning:

Fulfillment rate or simply the *fill rate* measures the ability of a supplying node to fulfill the demand placed on it. In its simplest term, this is the ratio of the quantity supplied over the quantity needed. A fill rate of 85% means that expected percentage of demand quantity fulfilled from stock is no less than 85% over the long run.

Service level primarily measures the ability of the supplier node to service the demand placed on it. This is typically a user input provided to the inventory optimization as a target value of service levels that is expected. Service level can also be thought of as the probability of a *stockout*. The probability of a stockout can be thought of as the probability that the inventory will be available when a demand is placed on a node. A service level of 92% can be interpreted either as (1) a guarantee that a positive inventory will be available at least 92 times out of 100; or as (2) a guarantee that at least 92% of the demand placed will always be fulfilled (fill-rate).

Inventory turns measure the efficiency of inventory deployment in the enterprise. This is computed as the ratio of the cost of goods sold over a year divided by the cost of average inventory during the same period. A higher value of the inventory turns signifies lower inventory holding costs, and generally requires a higher frequency of planning and ordering. All these factors together reduce the cost of inventory obsolescence and increase profitability. Inventory turns depend on various factors, such as the ordering frequency, inventory cover, safety stocks, expected service levels, supply lead-time, and order size. Most companies establish targets for the inventory turns based on their industry averages, though a careful analysis of the demand, supplies, lead-time, and ordering costs can also determine such targets.

Demand and supply variability are two parameters that are used in calculating optimal inventory levels at any node. Recall that any two nodes in a supply chain can be viewed as having a supplier–consumer relationship. In such a relationship, the demands are being placed by the consuming node on the supplier node, and supplies are flowing from the supplying node to the consuming node. The lists of these demand and supply quantities in time look like time series of random variables. The variability of the data in these time series measures the dispersion or spread of the numbers in the lists. This spread is important, because it provides a measure of the probability that the next number in the time series will be spread by a certain amount from the previous one. The variability affects the amount of inventory that must be maintained to ensure that service levels are met, and the probability of stockouts is predictable.

Variance is the statistical term that measures the variability.

Standard deviation is another statistical parameter that measures the spread of a series. This is computed as the *variance squared*.

Safety stock is the inventory that is specifically planned to be kept in stock as a buffer against the variability of demand and supply.

Cycle stock is sometimes used to denote the inventory required to cover the demand during the reorder period.

It is useful to review the two processes of replenishment and inventory planning together. The reordering or replenishment process defines the review period for reordering, and an ordering quantity. The inventory planning process establishes the safety stock and reorder levels for replenishment. Together these processes determine the inventory quantities to be maintained and replenished as well as the best time to do so.

In replenishment based on *continuous review*, the inventory levels are continuously reviewed, and as soon as the stocks fall below a predetermined level, usually called the *reorder point* or *reorder level*, a replenishment order is placed. As more and more companies start using sophisticated IT systems to track their inventories in real time, the continuous review method becomes a viable option to plan for replenishment.

In replenishment based on *periodic review*, the inventory levels are reviewed at a predefined frequency. At the time of review, if the stock levels are below this predetermined level, then an order for replenishment is placed; otherwise it is ignored until the next cycle. It provides an alternative to the continuous review method by segmenting the merchandise into review buckets. This makes it easier to manage when the process is manual, or the number of items involved is extremely large, or when constraints on ordering-day exist.

Two other terms relevant to the discussion are the *order quantity* and *order-up-to level (OUTL)*. Order quantity is simply a fixed quantity for ordering. If the replenishment process determines that an order should be placed, then the order for a predefined quantity for that item-location combination is placed for replenishment.

Alternatively, a predetermined order-up-to level can be defined. The actual order quantity is then determined as the difference between the on-hand stock on the review day, and the predetermined order-up-to level. The order quantity in this process will differ from one order to another depending on the on-hand quantity on the day of the review.

Using the review period options of continuous or periodic review, and the order quantity options of fixed order quantity or OUTL, the reordering

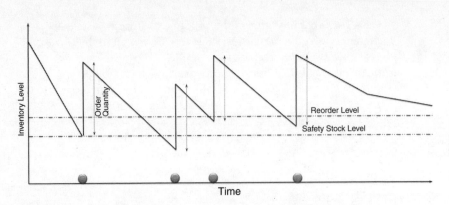

EXHIBIT 5.1 Order Point/Order Quantity/Continuous Review

process can be deployed in four basic ways. The diagrams in the exhibits depict the four variations of the reordering process:

1. *Order point/order quantity/continuous review.* This process uses a fixed "order quantity" with a continuous review. Exhibit 5.1 depicts the resulting process. To make it simpler, instantaneous replenishment is assumed. The orders are placed as soon as the inventory falls below the predetermined reorder levels, which are shown as the black dots. As the order quantity is fixed, the resulting inventory level after replenishment varies based on the starting inventory when the order is placed. The benefit of this approach is that it triggers an order as soon as the stocks fall below the reorder level, therefore rarely eating into the underlying safety stock layer. Orders are created when required and need to be managed as such.

2. *Order point/order quantity/periodic review.* This process is a variation of the first process, using a fixed "order quantity" but a periodic review. This is shown in Exhibit 5.2. The black dots in the diagram show the ordering points, and the gray dot shows a review when no order is placed as the inventory level is higher than the reorder level at the time of review. Note that the inventory may sometimes fall below the safety stocks before a replenishment order is placed. The benefit of this approach is a stable ordering cycle, though it does not guarantee inventory levels as well as the first approach.

3. *Order point/OUTL/continuous review.* This method, depicted in Exhibit 5.3, uses a predetermined OUTL for inventory to determine the size of the order. The inventory is reviewed continuously and orders placed as soon as the levels fall below the reorder level. The process targets to fill the inventory stocks to a predetermined level, and therefore the order size varies based on the on-hand inventory level.

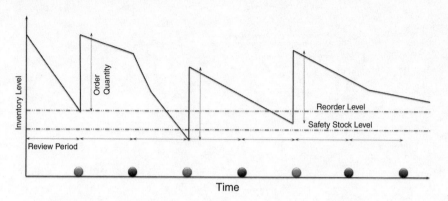

EXHIBIT 5.2 Order Point/Order Quantity/Periodic Review Replenishment

4. *Order Point/OUTL/periodic review.* This variation of reordering process, shown in Exhibit 5.4, uses an OUTL with a periodic review. Again, the order size varies from one to the next, and no order is placed if the inventory level at the time of review is higher than the predetermined reorder level.

Having reviewed these four processes, it is easier to explain that the objective of the inventory planning process is to establish the reorder and the safety stock levels. Inventory planning processes answer the following questions:

■ What is the optimal level of inventory to be maintained for the products carried at a location? What are the optimal safety stock and the reorder levels?

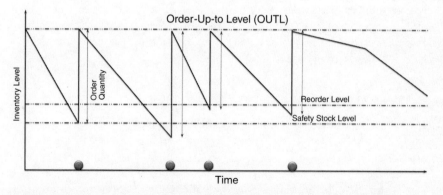

EXHIBIT 5.3 Order Point/Order-Up-to Level/Continuous Review Replenishment

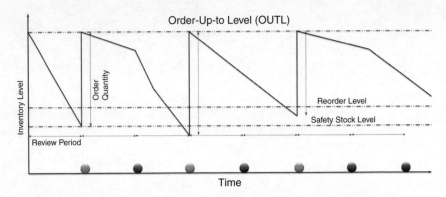

EXHIBIT 5.4 Order Point/Order-Up-to Level/Periodic Review Replenishment

- What service level can be guaranteed based on the suggested inventory levels?

These two parameters of safety stock and reorder levels control two of the most critical factors in a supply chain: the amount of inventory, and the ability to maintain favorable service levels.

As the demand and supply patterns change, the optimal inventory levels required to guarantee desirable service levels also change. Due to inherent variability in the demand and supply streams at any supply chain node, the ability to service demand directly depends on the safety stock. The relationship between the two is exponential, which means that a 100% guarantee to fulfill demand will, in theory, require an infinite amount of safety stock to be maintained. Exhibit 5.5 shows this relationship graphically.

A good inventory planning process helps define these levels, discriminating between products that require higher service levels and those that do not. It helps in maintaining user-defined service levels that guarantee desirable fill-rates to fulfill the demand. It also provides a process to review these parameters frequently to make changes to the safety stock recommendations to adjust to the new demand/supply picture.

Inputs and Outputs of the Inventory Planning Process

Inventory planning process needs the following inputs:

- Master data such as items/products, locations, planning horizon, and valid item-location combinations.
- Historical demand and supply data at each inventory carrying location where inventory stocking levels need to be computed.

- Supply lead-time history at the location acting as a supplier. This is the historical lead-time of the supplies. The lead-time may vary for every purchase order or transfer-order that is fulfilled, sometimes even for the same item. This time series provides the variability of the lead-time and helps the inventory optimization engine to determine the probability that a specific projected supply will be realized on the need date.
- Service level expected to be maintained at a location when it is acting as a supplier to another location in the supply chain.
- Inventory policy overrides by the user. For example, a user may override the periodic review policy or OUTL to take advantage of an extraordinary pricing opportunity offered by a vendor on a one-time basis.

The inventory planning applications normally preprocess the historical data for computing the variability and standard deviation for each product-location time series. Then they may employ different formulations to compute the optimal inventory levels, most of which are based on balancing the cost of stockouts and cost of holding inventory within the constraint of the expected service level specified by the user. A pictorial overview of the inventory planning process is shown in Exhibit 5.6.

The outputs of the inventory planning process are:

- Suggested inventory cover at a location for the target products. This can either be an absolute number that specifies the quantity of inventory to be maintained at the location or be specified in terms of number

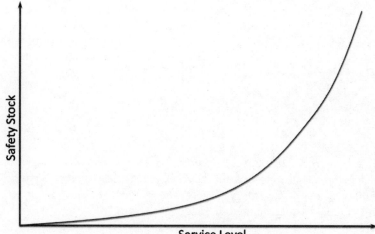

EXHIBIT 5.5 Service Level and Safety Stock

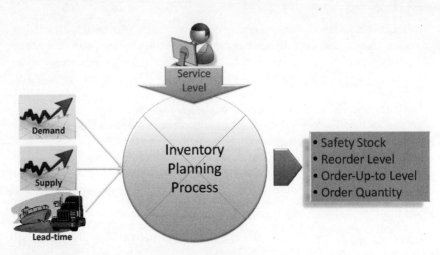

EXHIBIT 5.6 Inputs and Outputs of Inventory Planning

of days of inventory cover. The latter signifies the number of days of demand that the location will maintain as the safety stock.

- Reorder level and reorder quantities may be the other outputs of the process.

Related Subprocesses

Inventory planning as previously defined provides a decision-support system that helps users to define inventory levels sufficient to maintain a target service level at the location. However, the desired service levels will differ for different groups of products based on their demand, profitability, and product affinity attributes. There are other processes that help users determine what service levels should be maintained for which groups of locations and product combinations. Some of these are described here as the subprocesses of the inventory planning function.

INVENTORY CLASSIFICATION Inventory classification helps users to segregate products into more manageable groups with similar demand and supply characteristics. These groups are then managed together for setting up service-level targets, inventory targets, and other inventory policy parameters. This makes the maintenance and understanding of the master data simpler.

Inventory classification can be done using various techniques, from simple database queries to automated data mining and data discovery. The selected technique depends on the maturity of the users, data available, volume and quality of data, and complexity of the classification criteria.

Independent of the underlying technique, the users need to identify the attributes that are important to them in creating these inventory categories. Some of the relevant attributes will be demand patterns, average demand, demand velocity, and variability. Similar attributes for supply can be incorporated. Other factors to analyze could be profitability, cost of lost sales, and cost of stockouts, if available. Using these attributes and a user-specified range of values, the groups of products can be created. Each such group then needs to be profiled to establish its most prominent characteristics to understand, compare, and contrast with the other groups.

Simple database queries can create the inventory groups; however, as the number of variables increases, the number of such groups also increases. This may result in a large number of groups that are hard to understand and manage. Data discovery/mining–based solutions work better in such complex scenarios, where data volumes are large, many attributes relevant to classification exist, and the range of data values of these attributes may be unknown. Another advantage of using data mining solutions for inventory classification is that they can create the group profiles automatically to show the differentiating characteristics of the groups. However, such data mining–based solutions are complex and require specific skills to set up, configure, tune, and maintain. They may also require specialists with strong data mining and statistics backgrounds for successful adoption in the enterprise.

DEMAND AND SUPPLY PROPAGATION ACROSS SUPPLY CHAIN TIERS In multitier supply chain networks, independent demand occurs at the downstream locations that generally represent stores. Only this demand is relevant for statistical forecasting methods, because it is largely random and independent of any variables that are directly controlled. This is called the *independent demand*. Once the demand has been projected at this tier, it needs to be propagated across the network to upstream tiers that typically represent local and regional distribution centers, manufacturing plants, and vendor shipping locations. The propagated demand is then called *dependent demand* as this is derived from the independent demand and the supply chain network. This process helps in establishing demand to be fulfilled at each inventory-carrying node of the supply chain.

Similar to the demand propagation, the supplies are propagated in the supply chain models from the upstream end to the downstream end. This determines the projected supplies at each node of the chain.

Inventory planning uses these projected demand and supply numbers at each node for determining the optimal safety stock levels at these locations.

The propagation process requires that the supply chain network clearly identifies relationships among the consuming and supplying locations, stocking and service attributes for products at these locations, and lead-time parameters for the flows between the locations.

The simplest way to propagate demand and supply along the supply chain is *deterministic*, where each location with demand can be supplied by only a single supply location upstream. In such a case, the demand can be transferred to the upstream location simply by considering the transition lead-time.

However, real-life supply chains require more flexibility, and therefore are more complex to optimize. There may be more than one upstream location that can potentially fulfill a demand at a downstream location; there may be a bill-of-materials relationship between products at the upstream location and products at the demanding downstream location; the transition time to move products from one location to another may differ based on the mode of transport; costs of transfers may be different based on the selected supplying location; and resource constraints at the nodes and/or along the supply chain arcs may constrain otherwise-viable supplier–consumer relationships among the nodes.

Sophisticated supply chain solutions allow the users to propagate demand and supply in such complex scenarios using mathematical models that employ optimization techniques and/or *probabilistic* models to mimic the behavior of real supply chains and recommend solutions that are optimal as well as feasible to execute.

INVENTORY COSTS AND SERVICE-LEVEL SIMULATIONS A good inventory planning process should allow the users to assess the impact of their decisions on the inventory costs, and inventory turns *prior* to implementing these decisions. This calls for sophisticated analysis and scenario planning applications that support the main inventory calculations solution. It allows users to play with the service levels, and see the impacts of these changes on their inventory, serviceability, and costs before deciding on the target values.

Cost of inventory and inventory turns are two obvious metrics to evaluate each planned scenario; but total system costs consisting of cost of warehousing and transportation, ordering, and even cost of lost sales are quite relevant in evaluating these scenarios.

There are not many good commercially available tools for scenario planning and evaluation, and this may require a homegrown solution. Alternatively, a simpler analytics-based solution using generic analysis tools for comparison and analysis of various alternatives can be adopted as well.

Replenishment Planning

The demand forecast process produces unconstrained demand using the historical sales or consumption data. This unconstrained demand forecast needs to be converted to net demand. The difference between the unconstrained demand forecast and net demand forecast is that the net demand accounts for the inventories, and therefore produces a demand number that needs to be actually replenished for fulfilling the projected demand at a node. Net demand simply is the amount of new merchandise that must be purchased to fulfill the projected demand.

Replenishment planning considers the on-hand inventories, expected receipts (inbound inventory at a warehouse or store), and expected shipments (outbound inventory at the warehouse) for the planning period under consideration. Then net demand is simply the forecast demand minus on-hand minus expected receipts plus expected shipments.

In most cases, inventory safety stocks are maintained and this safety stock value is added to the above net demand number to ensure that the safety stocks are always available as planned. The safety stock calculations are provided by the inventory planning process described earlier, and are shown in Exhibit 5.7.

Further, replenishment planning may round off the numbers to conform to the supplier's fulfillment quantity constraints of minimum/maximum/ multiples, or to conform to internal process requirements. For example, if a supplier sells light bulbs in packs of 12, with 10 such packs in a box, then the supplier may constrain the orders to a minimum of one box (120 light bulbs) with the same multiple. Assuming that the warehouse breaks the boxes down into individual packs, then the warehouse will fulfill an order of a minimum of one pack or 12 light bulbs.

Supplier contracts may sometimes constrain the ordering quantities further, by requiring a minimum order quantity, a maximum order quantity, and a multiple of a given number (usually a case or box quantity that the supplier is unwilling to break). Similar constraints may be enforced for internal material transfers from a distribution center (DC) to the stores to enhance the DC productivity, so that the distribution centers do not have to break open pallets or cases. In the manufacturing world, it is not uncommon to have a minimum batch run on a production line before the setup is changed, and such batch-run quantities may constrain the order fulfillment

EXHIBIT 5.7 Unconstrained Demand Forecast and Net Demand

as well, where supplies are tied directly to the manufacturing operations. Some of these rounding constraints are shown in Exhibit 5.8.

This description for the replenishment planning process applies well to the forecasted demand. However, demand can originate through forecasts, allocation, or store requisitions created by inventory planners over and above the system projected demand. Replenishment planning consolidates all the demand streams together. This consolidated view of demand is used for determining the optimal fulfillment method.

One way to look at all these demands is to view them as requisitions for merchandise—whether they are created through forecasting (pull), allocation (push), or store users. The replenishment planning process takes all these requisitions as demand to be fulfilled. These requisitions may or may not have an identified supply source provided by the user or the originating system. If the supply source is not identified, then the fulfillment planning process will identify the supply source, and round up the fulfilled quantities to comply with flow constraints in the supply chain. These supply sources may be internal to a company's supply chain, or external.

For example, if the original requisition is for a store, the order fulfillment process may identify a specific warehouse for fulfilling the demand and change the fulfilled quantity to align with the fulfillment quantity constraints imposed by the warehouse. These constraints are usually the result of an established business practice or a rule that governs the warehouse operations for efficiency reasons. For example, a warehouse may break pallets into cases, but may not break cases into boxes or eaches. In this case, then, all orders fulfilled from the warehouse must be rounded to full cases. The number of eaches in a case will vary from item to item, and that provides the multiple for the fulfilled quantity that must be adhered to. In this case, the demand identified through the replenishment process is being fulfilled from a source internal to the company's supply chain. As the actual fulfillment transaction transfers merchandise between the two locations of the same corporation, this is considered a *transfer* in the financial world. Transfers result in financial reconciliation as assets move from one part of the corporation to another.

EXHIBIT 5.8 Rounding Factors for Net Demand

Consider another example where the demand is identified at a distribution center. This will potentially be fulfilled through a purchase order placed on a supplier that may be modeled as a supply node in the company's supply chain, even though it remains an external entity. These transactions will be managed through a purchase order lifecycle management system.

To summarize, the objective of the replenishment management process is to establish a consolidated demand picture for every node in the supply chain, which can drive the decisions for sourcing to fulfill this demand. Specifically it answers the following questions:

- What is the consolidated demand (quantity), where is this demand originating (location), and when does it need to be fulfilled (need date)?
- What does this demand consist of (how much of this demand exists due to the requirement to maintain safety stock, cycle stock, and so on)?
- How much inventory do I need at various points in the network to ensure that the demand at all the consuming nodes can be fulfilled?
- What are the best sources for fulfilling the above demand?
- What constraints must be considered to create feasible manufacturing, distribution, and purchase plans?
- Finally, what distribution (transfer) orders for warehouses, work orders for factories, and purchase orders for the vendors should be created and when?

The execution of the replenishment planning process in the supply chains primarily consists of the subprocesses of demand consolidation, source determination, and fulfillment planning, which are discussed next.

Demand Consolidation

This is the first step in the replenishment process. The requests for material requisitions can be created by multiple sources. The replenishment planning process needs to consolidate all demand requisitions. A consolidated view of demand at every location ensures that the best fulfillment solution can be obtained by considering all available inventory sources and transportation options.

Here are some of the sources of demand signals/requisitions for the replenishment planning process:

- The demand planning system can create these requisitions. These are based on the demand forecast. The replenishment plan created by using the demand forecasts is also called *pull-based replenishment*. The name comes from the fact that the demand history at the stores is generally used to create such demand forecast, and this demand then generates a pull on the merchandise in the warehouse, and as warehouse inventories go down they also create a pull on the suppliers. Of course, the forecasts actually provide a *simulated pull* to replenish, without which this will become reactive in nature, and extremely hard to manage.

- Another source of demand can be through the requisitions created by the inventory planners in the stores. As the inventory planners/managers in the stores are generally closest to the customer, they are also more aware of the inventory situation in the store. They should *ideally* have visibility into the replenishments suggested for their stores by the planning systems, and they can be allowed to either change those requisitions or create additional requisitions manually to supplement the planned replenishments. Without such visibility into the system-generated demand for the stores, these user-created requisitions can create overinventory situations rather quickly.

- One more source of demand is the requisitions from the merchants who might be planning to *push* merchandise into the stores. Merchants can decide to push the merchandise for various reasons. Some of the common ones are as follows:

  - *One-time buys*. The merchant can decide to buy a one-off assortment from a supplier at very low prices. Such deals can be a result of supplier closing off a line of merchandise, or a season coming to an end, or other similar situations. These one-time merchandise purchases can then be pushed out to the stores by the merchants through the same mechanism of requisitions.

  - *Seasonal buys*. Seasonal merchandise in some cases may not be planned using a demand forecasting process. In these situations, the merchant may simply decide the quantities, assortments, and dates when the merchandise will be pushed to the stores. Seasonal merchandise planning may also involve ramping up of the inventory at the warehouse at the start of the season, and ramping down at the end. Both these situations will result in allocation-based requisitions at the warehouses or the stores.

  - *Promotions and clearance*. Planned events like promotions and clearance can also result in push-based requisitions that are created either by the merchants or a centralized promotion planning or clearance application.

    This type of replenishment is called *push-based replenishment* because the merchandise is pushed to the stores in this case without the stores asking for the merchandise. This is also called *product allocation* or *allocation planning* by some application providers.

The demand consolidation process establishes the total demand originating at any supply chain node. While the demand at the most downstream

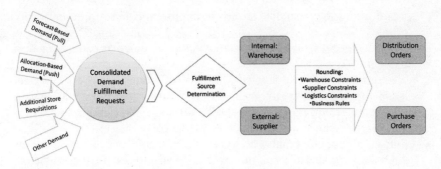

EXHIBIT 5.9 Demand Consolidation in Replenishment Planning

end of the supply chain is usually forecasted, the demand at other nodes is established by propagating this demand upstream through the network.

Fulfillment Planning and Source Determination

This process picks up after the demand consolidation is completed. Some of the replenishment applications may provide this functionality as an integrated step. The objective of this process is to review the consolidated demand and determine the optimal source of fulfillment, considering the inventory, lead-time, quantity-rounding constraints for fulfillment sizes and logistics, and create purchase order suggestions or distribution orders. Exhibit 5.9 shows a brief overview of the process.

Conventionally, this process uses a set of user-defined rules to select the best source. Optimization solutions for achieving the same function are qualitatively superior and help in reducing the total spend. However, the data requirements for such solutions are quite stringent and such solutions are still evolving.

The output of this process is outbound orders from warehouses to stores when the demand can be fulfilled from internal sources; work orders on manufacturing plans when the demand is fulfilled by manufacturing; or suggested purchase orders where such demand needs to be fulfilled from external suppliers.

For the purposes of coming up with feasible order quantities, the fulfillment quantities may be rounded up or down to allowed multiples and minimum and maximum quantity constraints. The rounding can use several possible criteria. Some of the examples for rounding the replenishment quantities are presented here:

- Supplier contracts (e.g., minimum order quantity/value).
- Warehouse constraints (minimum quantity based on the smallest package down to which the warehouse will break a pallet).

- Manufacturing constraints based on minimum batch-run quantity on a specific setup.
- Logistics considerations (rounding up to create a truckload or container).
- Other organizational constraints, such as minimum order value derived from the ordering cost considerations for the enterprise. The concept of *economic order quantity (EOQ)* is based on balancing the cost of holding inventory against the cost of ordering. The newer algorithms for determining optimal order quantities can consider extended parameters and dynamically compute the order size based on several factors, including the above two factors, and supply contracts, cost of lost sales, and demand and supply probabilities.

When the identified supply source is internal to the enterprise supply chain, such as a warehouse or a manufacturing plant, the transaction mechanism to fulfill the demand is often called a *transfer note*, a *distribution order*, or a *work order*. A distribution order basically directs a warehouse to ship the required merchandise to a store or another warehouse. A work order directs the factory to manufacture the authorized merchandise.

When all the potential sources are internal, the cost of transfer of material is typically not a huge consideration in selection of the best source to fulfill the demand. While some corporations may model a different cost of transfer among their own facilities for internal transfers, most of the retailers use standard costing or other similar inventory-valuation methods for such transfers that are consistent across internal facilities. Another difference for internal transfers is that they may have greater flexibility in terms of quantities that can be shipped from these warehouses to the stores. While most suppliers have minimum and maximum order quantities that must be met on the purchases being made, the internal transfers are subject to ship packs at the warehouses with the warehouse manager able to make exceptions if required. Therefore, the sourcing optimization for internal sources becomes an easier process that may not be required to consider the cost and shipping-quantity constraints.

However, other factors such as transportation costs, need dates, leadtime, and warehouse capacities are some of the variables that should be taken into account for determining the best internal source of supplies.

When the identified source is an external supplier, then the transaction to execute the fulfillment is called a *purchase order*. A purchase order acts as a formal contract between the enterprise and the supplier for the exchange of goods and services for monetary consideration.

When there are multiple external suppliers who can potentially fulfill the current demand, it presents another opportunity for optimization and cost savings. These suppliers may have contracts in place with negotiated price tiers, discounts, and volume rebates. In such cases, the cost of material can differ based on the current order volumes; historical purchase volumes; contractual obligations and current status; season; and price, rebates, and discount tiers. The cost of shipping affects the cost of transportation, and depends on the supplier warehouse location from where the order will be fulfilled. All these factors affect the landed cost of purchase. Other parameters such as need dates, lead-time, and the warehouse capacities are still relevant and should be considered in pursuit of an optimal solution. Due to the long-term contractual obligations in this scenario, even the future projected demand can be considered to determine the optimal purchase plan to reduce the total cost of purchases without affecting the ability to fulfill all planned demand.

However, the existing packaged supply planning solutions do not support modeling these costs to determine the optimal supply sources. They typically model a deterministic supply model where the supplier–consumer relationships are rigidly defined. When these solutions allow modeling of multiple choices for such supplies, they constrain the selection through a primary or default supply location that switches to an alternative location only when one of the predefined conditions is violated. For example, a typical solution may always use the defined primary source of supply unless this location is out of inventory, in which case a user-provided alternative location is used. This type of deterministic behavior of the models depends on arbitrary user input, does not allow cost modeling, and therefore is unable to provide an optimal, cost-aware solution.

Inputs and Outputs of the Replenishment Planning Process

The replenishment planning process needs the following inputs:

- Master data such as items/products, locations, planning horizon, and valid item-location combinations. The item-location combination is also called *assortment*, especially when used in the context of a retail store.
- Demand through all channels (pull, push, user created, etc.) that needs to be fulfilled.
- On-hand inventory and expected receipts and shipments of inventory.
- Inventory policies (e.g., safety stock/cover).
- Inventory flow constraints between the nodes (minimum, maximum, multiples) that must be met. These constraints can come from suppliers, logistics, and user business rules.
- Valid supplier–product relationships, supplier contracts, supplier warehouse locations, and shipping costs if landed cost calculations can be leveraged by the process. In case of manufacturing, factories and prod-

ucts they can produce, production capacities, and manufacturing calendar will all become required inputs to the process.
- Lead-time for replenishment, which may consist of procurement lead-
time or manufacturing lead-time.

The process then calculates the net requirements at each node and
rounds them off to comply with the inventory flow parameters between the
supplying and receiving node. It provides the following output:

- Demand to be replenished at a node corresponding to the projected
demand forecast for the specified time horizon
- Fulfillment plan by way of suggested orders for suppliers, factories, and
distribution orders for warehouses

Related Subprocesses

Replenishment planning needs safety stocks that must be maintained at the
supplying nodes to maintain guaranteed service levels. These safety stock
calculations are typically provided by the inventory planning process, which
was covered in this chapter prior to the replenishment planning section.

Production Planning

The production planning process helps align the manufacturing resources
with the demand in the supply chain that has been identified to be fulfilled
through the factory orders. The production planning process at this level
reviews the demand of the finished goods to be fulfilled and establishes the
raw material and manufacturing capacity requirements. It then lays out the
two in discrete time buckets to create a high-level production plan.

The conventional production planning processes consisted of creating
production and capacity plans at different levels of abstraction and reconciling them to create a feasible plan. Examples of these processes are
aggregate production plan and *resource requirements plan, master production schedule (MPS), rough-cut capacity planning (RCCP),* and finally, *material requirements planning (MRP)* and *capacity requirements planning
(CRP).* Later enhancements to these functions, collectively called *manufacturing requirements planning (MRP II),* created closed-loop feedback
between the material and capacity plans to produce better quality plans.

The advanced production planning that is prevalent today differs from
these processes in that it considers the actual constraints on the available material and capacity simultaneously to produce feasible production plans that
do not require any reconciliation unless the inventory or resource positions

have changed. In fact, the advanced planning process for manufacturing is a microcosm of the larger supply chain itself as it involves modeling operations, resources, and material movement along nodes and flow-paths that model their own inventory behavior, process, material, and flow (throughput) constraints.

Currently available solutions allow modeling of a large number of constraints to represent manufacturing operations. In Exhibit 5.10, modeled for a pen manufacturer, the forecasts and orders pull the finished goods from the warehouse. The warehouse node represented in this exhibit can be modeled with inventory policies for acting as a supplier to the orders, and as a consumer "pulling" pens from the upstream process. Each process in turn transmits the demand to the next upstream element in the supply chain that must respond to this demand.

In the role of a supplier, a node can model its response behavior in many possible ways. It can immediately address the demand as it originates in the exact same quantity as asked. If standard lot sizes for demand exist, this will represent a lot-for-lot behavior at this node. The node can wait until it has accumulated enough demand signals to fill a truck and then respond. While the downstream nodes may have to wait, this could produce overall cost efficiencies. A node can simply have a calendar to model the ship-days; for example, all demand is shipped only on Mondays, and so on.

Similarly, a node in its role as a consumer can model different behaviors to reflect real-life situations. For example, it may not create any demand on its upstream element until it reaches a predefined reorder level. When this level is reached, it may round up the demand to an OUTL quantity, or use a fixed order quantity. Or it may simply act in a lot-for-lot fashion and ask for replenishments for each shipment it makes.

Operations in the model also behave in a predefined manner to reflect the real-life constraints. For example, an operation may need a worker that has a work schedule with predefined work time and holidays. Operations may model resources with specific skills or specific machining requirements. Operations take time, and they can also model setup changes when the production run for a specific product is completed and the manufacturing line setup needs to be changed to a different product.

Some of these elements are shown in Exhibit 5.10, for a pen manufacturer that has the receiving operation for the raw material, polypropylene, followed by the molding operations to manufacture caps and bodies. The refills for the pens are supplied by another factory that works with a request–promise mechanism to respond to the pen manufacturer's assembly operation plans. The *request and promise* mechanism models a collaborative relationship between two supply chains, where one supply chain continuously shares the emerging demand picture with the other, which responds

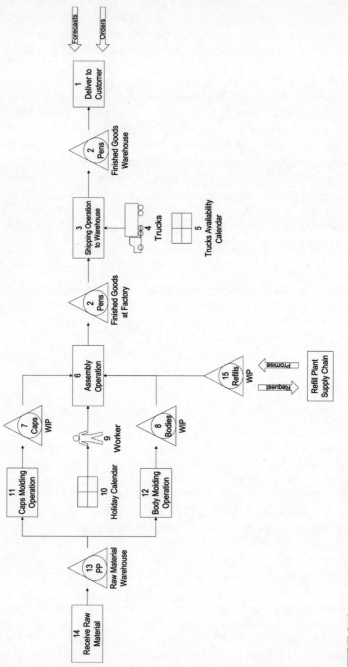

EXHIBIT 5.10 Example of a Pen Manufacturing Model

with a promise to fulfill the projected demand. The pens after assembly are sent to a finished-goods warehouse that is stocked to respond to firm customer orders, as well as forecast-based demand. Notice that some operations in Exhibit 5.10, such as operations 11 and 12, representing molding capacity, do not have any constraints, while the assembly operation 6 has resource constraints modeled through a calendar. When a production sequence has a number of operations, the total throughput of the production sequence is generally constrained by the operation that has the least throughput. Therefore, it may suffice to simply model this constraint rather than modeling all capacity constraints.

At this level, the advanced production planning process models the manufacturing process at an abstract level that does not represent every physical asset. For example, the molding operation shown as a single bucket of capacity may actually consist of a few plastic molding machines of different types and capacities while the model represents their cumulative capacity. Similar abstraction can be applied to represent the total transportation capacity and the stocking capacity of a facility.

To develop production plans at different levels of abstraction, similar models can be developed representing these assets at required levels of granularity to produce operation plans that closely reflect the manufacturing process and facilities.

Some of the industry terms related to the production planning process are described below.

A bill of materials (BOM) refers to the definition of the components of a product, and a simple example of a BOM is depicted in Exhibit 5.11. In the pen manufacturing example, the bill of materials will show that the pen consists of the body, cap, and a refill. This is level 1 of the BOM. Refill in turn may consist of a tube and ink, which represents level 2 of the BOM. Bills of materials also have the quantity information, and may have substitution information when such options exist. When the product design changes, affecting the BOM, an *engineering change notice (ECN)* is used to communicate and manage such changes.

Bill of resources (BOR) is sometimes used to refer to the definition of resources required for an operation. Just as operations need materials that are defined by the BOM, they also need resources that are represented through the bill of resources. A bill of resources tells about not only the resources required by an operation but also the quantity and substitution options for such a resource.

Routing or *production routing* is the sequence of operations that is required for manufacturing or assembling a product or subassembly.

Work in progress (WIP) refers to the inventory of components and subassemblies that are part of the production process and represent goods that have not yet been finished for selling. Manufacturing typically looks at the materials in three distinct buckets as raw materials, WIP, and finished goods. Raw materials are the inputs that are required to produce the finished goods, and the material during this transition is called *WIP*.

Lot-for-lot represents an inventory policy where an inventory location responds to fulfill a demand and immediately raises the same demand on its upstream inventory location. These inventory locations then do not typically have large inventory stock as they simply act as pass-through for the demand signals. A similar policy can be defined for a manufacturing station as well. Defining a larger lot size reduces volatility in the system by reducing the number of supply requests created, or in a manufacturing situation by reducing the number of setup changes, but it also places artificial constraints on the demand and supply equations, and requires higher inventory to be maintained. Ability to define a lot size of 1 provides an ideal situation as it allows supply requests in any possible quantity and does not require any artificial rounding that may result in unwanted inventory at the node. But maintaining a lot size of 1 may introduce system volatility due to too many set-up changes or material requisitions and drive down the operational efficiency. Therefore, maintaining a lot size of 1 may not be feasible or even desirable to

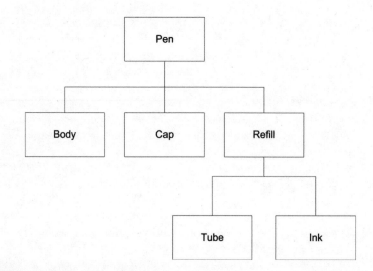

EXHIBIT 5.11 Simple Bill of Materials

maintain plan stability and operational efficiency. Hence, lot sizes are computed to be optimal for a given situation. For manufacturing operations, the cost of set-up change is balanced against the cost of carrying inventory, while for purchasing operations; the cost of ordering is balanced against the cost of carrying inventory to determine optimal lost size.

In a manufacturing situation, flexibility in defining the lot size will allow any quantity to be manufactured before changing the setup for a different product. In theory, if a lot size of 1 can be obtained for a manufacturing station, then any quantity can be manufactured on that station before changing the setup for another product. This assumes that the setup change time is zero or close to zero. In practice, manufacturing lot size is constrained by the cost of changing the setup for the next batch. Setup costs consist of the skilled labor required to set up a manufacturing station for production of a different article. These costs may further include staging raw material and subassemblies, and setting up inspection and quality assurance facilities for this production batch. These setup costs are generally fixed in nature whether the production batch size is small or large. Therefore, higher setup costs normally require a larger batch to drive down the setup cost per piece of production.

Advanced planning systems (APS) is the collective name of the planning applications that leverage constraint-based planning, simultaneously considering the material, capacity, and process constraints to create feasible production plans.

Planning horizon refers to the overall period for which the plans are created. For example, this may well be a year for aggregate planning processes, or just a few weeks for an operational planning process. The planning horizon is further divided into smaller periods, each known as a *planning bucket*. For example, a planning horizon spanning a year may have planning buckets of months.

Planning fence refers to a distinct time identified along the plan horizon for a specific purpose. For example, one may define a frozen fence at four weeks for an aggregate production plan to signify that no changes can be made within those four weeks to provide a stable production schedule.

Stockout typically refers to the inventory situation when the on-hand stock reaches zero, or a predefined level where the node is incapable of fulfilling any demand placed on it.

Order pegging is the practice of identifying the manufacturing work orders for specific sales or demand orders so that the status of any sales order can be precisely tracked through the manufacturing or fulfillment process.

The advanced production planning process answers the following questions for the enterprise's plan horizon:

- Are there enough material and capacity to address the projected demand? What are the raw material requirements? What are the resource requirements? Are the resources leveled? Is it feasible to achieve the projected sales plan with the current resource capacity?
- What orders will be fulfilled on time? Are there any orders that will be delayed or cannot be fulfilled as received?
- If order-pegging functions are used, then what is the status of a specific order in the manufacturing process?

Inputs and Outputs of the Production Planning Process

The production planning process needs the following inputs:

- Demand plan that needs to be addressed, with quantities and need dates. This demand may be a combination of various demand components such as forecast, customer orders, and demand for inventory layers (such as safety stock).
- Bill of materials, bill of resources, and routing information for all finished goods for which the demand exists. The routing information would have the process lead-time and setup lead-time required to change a workstation from producing one part/subassembly to another.
- Projected availability of raw materials and WIP and resources such as machinery and labor.
- Order or demand priorities.

This information is used to model the production process, with constraints on inventory, resources, and process sequence. The planning process then proceeds through the propagation of demand upstream within the modeled constraints of inventory, resources, process, and need dates of the orders. The orders with higher priority are processed first to give them the best possible opportunity at the materials and resources.

The output of the master production planning process is as follows:

- The daily production schedule, which is a schedule of production operations with start and end times, resources and material used, and output produced
- The purchase schedule for the raw materials with the material required, and the quantity, date, and location where it is required

Logistics Capacity Planning

Logistics capacity planning is focused on longer-term transportation and warehousing capacity planning. It consists of analyzing the current and projected needs for transportation and warehousing based on the enterprise's business plans for the future.

The following processes cover the transportation capacity planning and procurement and the warehouse capacity planning. The transportation planning process ensures that enough capacity is available under contract with the carriers on the projected routes/lanes to address the changing demands of shipping between suppliers, factories, warehouses, and stores. The warehousing capacity planning ensures that there is enough warehousing capacity to stock the projected inventory levels to serve the planned future business volumes. Warehouses have a long lead-time for setup and operations, and this capacity planning exercise allows the enterprise to be proactive as warehousing needs change.

Transportation Capacity Planning

As part of the strategic and long-term growth plans, transportation capacity planning processes provide the projected growth in the transportation requirements of the company. This is more important in distribution-intensive industry verticals such as retail, as the transportation costs in the retail industries can be a substantial part of the sales revenues. Planning the logistics capacity for warehousing and transportation requirements ahead of time allows for an optimally planned network that is geared to support the growth in merchandise volumes and stores.

Transportation capacity planning processes answer the following questions:

- What are the projected needs for transportation capacity to support the corporate growth goals?
- What is the best way to address these needs (modes/lanes/routes)?

INPUTS AND OUTPUTS OF THE TRANSPORTATION CAPACITY PLANNING PROCESS
Transportation capacity planning needs the following information as inputs:

- Future network model of the supply chain. This network may consist of existing and planned stores, warehouses, factories, and major vendor locations.
- Projected transportation volume and mode requirements along the supply chain arcs in the projected network.

- Current shipping data, volumes, rates/routes/lanes, costs, equipment types, modes, carrier capacities, carrier contracts.

The process primarily consists of analyzing the current and projected shipping volumes along each existing route/lane, projected requirements by mode, projected costs, budgets or targets, and available and expiring contract capacities. It provides the basic output as follows:

- New route and lane requirements
- Shipping volume requirements by mode (ocean/air/rail/road)
- Carrier selection guidelines
- Projected volume requirements along existing and new routes, existing contracted capacities, and gaps by mode

Transportation Capacity Procurement

These processes refer to the carrier bidding, evaluations, and contract awards. Transportation procurement is generally a well-established process for most retailers, as expected in any distribution-intensive industry. It is also a prime process for subcontracting due to industry-wide standardized communication messages and established business practices.

The process takes inputs from the transportation capacity planning function and generates bids. Carriers can be invited to respond to the bids and responses are evaluated for costs, capacities, lanes offered, equipment available, committed capacity, and other factors that may be relevant, such as financial stability of the carrier. The contracts are then awarded to the selected carriers for selected lanes.

The process and strategy for obtaining the capacity for domestic carriers for rail/road transport will be very different from planning for ocean-carrier capacity for international freight. For both of these requirements, some capacity may be contracted/dedicated and other capacity can be obtained from the open market at the actual time of need.

The actual requirement for transportation capacity will vary depending on product demand cycles, holidays, and seasons. Such fluctuations are normal and expected. These are fulfilled with a combination of contractual and dedicated capacity that is purchased in advance, and finally by buying the capacity on demand from the open market.

This process primarily addresses the following questions:

- Which carriers should be used for fulfilling the current and short-term projected transportation needs? What modes and equipment types are ideal? How much of this must be dedicated capacity?

- How much of the above capacity requirements are covered by existing contracts, and where do the gaps exist?
- What will it cost?

INPUTS AND OUTPUTS OF THE TRANSPORTATION CAPACITY PROCUREMENT PROCESS Transportation capacity procurement needs the following information as inputs:

- Current and projected transportation volumes by mode and equipment type, along lanes/routes
- Current contracts, committed capacities, expiration dates, and gaps in the required and available capacity for each lane
- Target carriers to be invited for tendering (especially when the carriers are required to be short-listed based on other overriding criteria such as corporate status, financial status, credit rating, etc.)

The process consists of publishing the bids on a portal, or via other methods, and inviting carriers to respond. The responses are then evaluated and compared using a predefined criterion that may include carrier costs, accessorial charges, available equipment, available lanes, process automation, prior relationships, and carrier historical performance for on-time delivery, tender acceptance rates, and any other criteria important to the corporation, such as financial viability. Contracts are awarded based on these comparisons. The output of the process is then:

- New and/or renewed carrier contracts to address the transportation capacity needs
- Analysis of the projected transportation capacity requirements, and fulfillment plans

Warehouse Capacity Planning

Like transport capacity planning, the strategic and long-term growth plans should cover the projected growth in the warehousing requirements of the company. This is another process that is important in distribution-intensive industry verticals to ensure that the warehousing growth is aligned with the planned business growth. As setting up a physical warehouse may take a long time, in some cases up to three years, planning for the warehousing capacity ahead of time helps maintain an optimal network to support the growth in merchandise volumes and stores.

Warehouse strategy is closely related to the network planning process. A whole host of other factors go into the warehouse location selection even after the warehouse capacities have been planned and optimal locations have been identified using a network planning solution. Such factors involve diverse decision inputs, ranging from demographics to average salaries in the target area, skills, local taxes, and government attitudes, and are not always quantifiable. This process here refers only to the quantifiable inputs for the purposes of capacity planning.

Warehouse capacity planning processes answer the following questions:

- What are the projected needs for warehousing capacity to support the corporate growth goals?
- What is the best way to address these needs? Where should these warehouses be? What types of warehouses should these be? What flow-paths should they support, and what level and type of mechanization should be planned at these facilities?

INPUTS AND OUTPUTS OF THE WAREHOUSING CAPACITY PLANNING PROCESS

Warehouse capacity planning needs the following information as inputs:

- Current and planned network models of the supply chain
- Projected storage volume; receiving, shipping, and flow-through expectations in the projected network
- Current warehouse capacities for storage and warehouse operations
- Level of mechanization, merchandise attributes, and volumes, (conveyable and nonconveyable)

The process primarily consists of analyzing the current and projected storage volumes, and the transaction volumes for receiving, shipping, and flow-through requirements. It provides the basic output as:

- Warehousing storage requirements and recommended levels of automation to support the projected transaction volumes; recommendations on the type of facility (cross-docking, stocking)
- Projected throughput requirements for various warehousing activities required to support the future distribution models, and volumes

Summary

The objective of the supply planning processes in supply chain management is to create replenishment plans that adequately and optimally address demand at every node of the chain. To achieve this objective, these processes use inventory planning functions that determine the optimal inventory levels for a target service level, and replenishment planning functions that further refine the replenishment requirements so that they are compliant with the sourcing constraints.

Inventory planning algorithms use demand and supply historical data, along with the lead-time for fulfillment and target service level, to establish optimal levels of inventory to be maintained at the supply chain nodes. This helps reduce inventory expense in the supply chains. Inventory classification can help managers in defining target service levels objectively.

Different combinations of order point, order quantity, and frequency of review allow the companies to create several replenishment scenarios that can be used for different types of material. The source determination for replenishment is another critical function of this process, as these sources can be internal or external.

When the fulfillment sources are internal manufacturing plants, production planning may be included as part of the extended supply planning process. Production planning establishes the production schedules and drives raw material purchases.

As the objective of the supply planning processes is to create replenishment plans that are optimal and feasible, logistics planning is presented as part of the process. When logistics constraints such as the shipping capacity between two nodes are real, the supply plans must be constrained to ensure feasibility. Therefore, an integrated approach to create supply plans should establish optimal inventory levels and replenishment requirements, identify fulfillment sources, and also account for the stocking and transportation constraints for satisfying demand at every node of the supply chain.

PART III

Supply Chain Execution

CHAPTER 6

Supply Management

The supply management functions of a supply chain have a large scope from sourcing to purchasing, manufacturing, replenishment, and vendor performance management. This is the other side of the demand equation, and consists of everything that needs to be done to fulfill the demand.

On a broader level, there are two aspects of supply management functions. The first deals with supply management functions, examples of which are determining the best sources for merchandise, the procurement of the merchandise, and global trade. The second part of the supply management functions deals with the suppliers themselves and managing the relationship with them. All of these functions will be discussed in the following sections.

Strategic Sourcing

The strategic sourcing process consists of finding out the best sources of supply, determining the feasibility of a strong and lasting relationship with the vendor, and managing this relationship over time to mutual benefit and advantage. The "strategy" in the strategic sourcing comes from proactive trend management to ensure that projected business plans and demands can be fulfilled with *adequate supplies, optimal costs,* and *minimal regulatory, financial, social (brand), and legal risks.*

As part of strategic sourcing, companies need to establish what they will need in the future and how much. This question is generally answered in the merchandising functions using the product portfolio analysis, profitability analysis, and other such techniques. Once the *what* and *how much* questions are addressed, strategic sourcing kicks in to establish *where* such needs may be optimally fulfilled.

The strategic sourcing processes consist of establishing guidelines for partnerships, creation and maintenance of approved vendor lists, procedures for on-boarding and off-boarding, vendor performance tracking, and partner compliance with the negotiated agreements, expectations, and behavior.

Partner Evaluation and On-boarding

Retailers deal with thousands of suppliers to replenish their warehouses and stores. Ever-expanding store assortments only increase the number of active suppliers at any point in time. Manufacturers also need a predictable supplier base to guarantee raw material supplies without interruption to ensure efficient utilization of their resources and ability to service their customers reliably. Partner evaluation establishes a consistent process to determine whether a potential supplier-partner will be a good fit.

Several considerations go into this decision, and some of the primary ones are as follows:

- *Financial considerations*. Financial health of the prospective partner is important for various reasons. Most important among them are the potential partners' ability to finance the merchandise order placed on them, staying solvent through the payment period, and being there for any product/warranty claims. This becomes more and more important in a global marketplace where lead-times are longer, and merchandise is sold in many continents, creating a widespread user base that then requires service and help.

   For publicly traded companies, such information may be available in the public domain. It can also be obtained from data providers that maintain such corporate data, update it at regular intervals, and sell the information for a price. These data providers can supply data on current operations, cash-flows, creditworthiness, lawsuits, business plans, and executives. It is not unusual for corporations to establish thresholds for each relevant attribute that their partners must pass to do business with them.

- *Assortment considerations* answer some basic questions. Does the partner have what the retailer needs? Does the assortment supplied by the partner have any unique selling points that can be leveraged? Should this be an exclusive supply relationship? Is the assortment deep, or wide? What is the quality of the assortment? What types of returns history does the partner have for similar assortment?

- *Legal and social considerations*. This aspect of evaluation ensures that it is legal to deal with the prospective partner and that their social positioning is agreeable to the retailer's image. Governments and other regulatory agencies routinely publish lists of blacklisted countries, corporations, and individuals. Corporations based in the home country of such governments may not be permitted to do business with those on the blacklists.

- *Social and cultural considerations* affect the brand and the corporate image (think of a corporation importing shoes or carpets from a country where child labor is prevalent). Such associations can be expensive and may be part of the corporate evaluation for selecting partners.
- Finally, considerations such as the manufacturing facilities, capacities, currency regulations, process certifications (e.g., ISO 9000 compliance), technology (e.g., ability of the partner to communicate using EDI messages), and communication (linguistic barriers) may be additional parameters in selecting partners.

Partner evaluation and on-boarding typically takes the form of a long collaborated information exchange either through paper forms, or increasingly through a Web portal. The datafeeds from third-party corporate data providers are also added to the data provided by the supplier. The host corporation can review the data to decide whether a supplier passes its partnership credentials.

The next step in the on-boarding process may require additional tasks of certifying vendor processes that will be common for all business communication, such as commonly transacted EDI messages, and setting up the high-level partner terms (or a master contract), which might cover things like payment terms, transit insurance, price basis, and returns, and so on.

INPUTS AND OUTPUTS OF THE PARTNER EVALUATION AND ON-BOARDING PROCESS

As described earlier, the partner evaluation process can be very specific to a corporation. There are no standard or "right" inputs or parameters to evaluate a partner. This is a process that needs to be customized to identify evaluation parameters for partners that are relevant to a corporation, for instance:

- Financial parameters, such as credit rating, operating cash-flow, balance sheet, profit and loss (P&L), projected growth versus industry, financial ratios, and other standard financial information to determine the financial health, growth prospects, and creditworthiness of the company
- Legal parameters, such as ability to do business with the host country, past and current lawsuits for product liability, intellectual property, or poor service, and any other indicators that may show the company's service record for honoring contractual obligations
- Social parameters, like brand image in home country, manufacturing facilities, manufacturing accidents and compensation history, worker welfare programs, worker unions, and worker rights

- Product and process quality inputs, international accreditations, and events such as product recalls, other quality issues, and process capabilities

The output of a successfully completed vendor evaluation process is an approved and on-boarded partner. However, if the prospective partner did not successfully comply with the requirements of the evaluation process, then the partnership will be denied. Successful vendors are typically added to the approved vendor list of the enterprise, allowing the business systems to transact with the new partners.

RELATED SUBPROCESSES   A process that closely supports the partner evaluation and on-boarding is the maintenance of *approved vendor lists (AVLs)*. Larger corporations specifically need to have a clearly defined and controlled process for defining and complying with the criteria for selecting, maintaining, and updating the list of vendors with which the corporation will do business. Having a well-defined standard for selecting partners reduces organizational risk of discriminatory practices and provides everyone involved in the process with a common measure.

An AVL can be viewed as a master list of corporate partners that may include suppliers, carriers, or service providers. Many of the corporate applications validate transactional data with this list prior to creating or settling a transaction. For example, the purchasing applications may restrict placing purchase orders only on the suppliers that are on the corporate AVL.

AVLs may incorporate review at predefined intervals where the AVL suppliers' data is updated and validated against the current corporate standards for partnerships. Such reviews are also triggered by events such as a contract renewal with an existing supplier.

Suppliers may be retired from the AVL if they do not meet the criteria, or where the need for doing business no longer exists, or due to poor service/performance.

Many ERP and master data applications provide functionality that supports definition, creation, and maintenance of AVLs.

Bidding and Contracts

The bidding and contracts process addresses the need to have stable sources and terms of supplies. It covers bid creation, tendering, analysis, and awards. Once the contracts are in place, the process enables tracking of compliance with the contracts and of outstanding obligations and provides alerts on contracts that need renewal.

Contracts reduce the risk of supply and costs fluctuations and help stabilize the supply chain processes. The objectives and terms of a contract can vary widely, and depend on the demand and supply profiles of the merchandise. Not all purchases require a long-term supply contract in place. Examples of product categories suitable for long-term contracts are exclusive merchandise with branding agreements, hard-to-obtain merchandise, seasonal merchandise, merchandise with stable high-volume demand, and so on.

The following describes the typical steps involved in creating, evaluating, and negotiating the bids to establish long-term supply contracts.

The first step after the merchandise for bidding has been selected is the preparation of the bid. The bidding process can be a single-step process where the buyer specifies the requirements, and suppliers can provide the product and service information as well as terms of supply. This is generally called a *request for quotation (RFQ)*. Alternatively, bidding can be a multi-step process with a *request for information (RFI)* calling for product information that is used by the buyer to put together its requirements, followed by a *request for proposal (RFP)*. The RFP then details the terms of supply.

In all cases, having a standard definition for the process and the templates for the RFx makes the bidding process easier, repeatable, and effective. Standard templates with predefined terms and conditions also allow for a larger group of buyers to interact with suppliers without the need to have all such interactions reviewed for legal vulnerabilities.

The next step in the process consists of identifying the target list of suppliers that will be asked to participate in the bidding process. It can be an open bid, which means that all suppliers are invited to participate, or a bid by invitation that is generally restricted to a short list of suppliers selected by the buyer. Open bids may require the supplier evaluation and on-boarding process if the winning supplier is not on the AVL.

Once the list of suppliers has been identified, the bid is published on an interactive portal or sent to them for response.

Bid responses follow the published bids. Standard bidding templates may also aid in receiving responses that are easier to understand and compare. It is not uncommon to have the bid responses electronically submitted in an online portal environment where the buyers can force standard formats for such proposals. Either way, these responses need to be compared and evaluated.

One of the best methods for evaluating bids is to calculate the total landed cost for each of the proposals. Better yet, total cost over the proposed lifecycle of the contract provides a good view of their relative standing. The latter requires projected future demand for the merchandise in question with some level of confidence.

Bid evaluation applications can enable such comparisons, especially when the proposals have many parameters, such as multiple shipping points (thus affecting the landed costs) or tiered pricing structures, rebates and discounts, and so on, which make it harder to compute the total landed cost for the contract lifecycle demand.

Bid negotiations may follow with a short list of suppliers. Most often, two or three suppliers are selected for the final rounds of negotiations. Such negotiations may cover all aspects of the contracts, such as price structures, rebates, discounts, surcharges, shipping, transit insurance, payment and credit terms, quality, process metrics, fulfillment and process time guarantees, service, cost of returns and returns-handling process, ordering and shipping parameters, and any other factors that may be important to the buyer or the supplier. Once the negotiations are successfully concluded, the contract is awarded to the supplier and becomes a valid contract against which purchases can now be made.

The contracts are tracked for performance, compliance, and obligations throughout their life. Such compliance can be a proactive process that prevents noncompliant transactions, or can be a reactive process that simply tracks such deviations and reports on them after the fact. This process manages the contract through its whole lifecycle until the contract is completed, canceled, terminated, or renewed.

Most of the contract management applications provide parts of the functionality to support this process. Commonly supported functionality includes an online interactive portal environment for RFx, responses, comparisons, and awards. Some solutions also allow document management and actual contract creation through the same online portal.

The bid optimization process that allows the buyers to understand the lifetime cost impacts of their contract decisions is not very common, and often involves a separate software application that needs IT help for data integration and reporting. Some vendors offer hosted services for bid optimization. It is still a relatively emerging application and requires sophisticated buyers who understand their demand patterns well and can provide contract proposals and the demand data for such systems to work.

Finally, a few of the available contract management solutions track purchases made against a contract and can create reports on noncompliant transactions, missed service levels, incorrect pricing/invoices, cumulative purchases, remaining obligations, and potential rebates. However, there are currently no packaged applications that proactively leverage contracts to manage the complete purchasing lifecycle. Potential savings exist by optimizing the purchase plans that leverage contracts and pricing structures when the long-term demand is known.

INPUTS AND OUTPUTS OF THE BIDDING AND CONTRACTS PROCESS   Bidding and contract management process needs vary largely due to the multitude of potential parameters and processes that are possible for achieving the targeted business objectives. Some of the common inputs are as follows:

- Historic and projected demand, demand patterns, and landed costs for raw material or merchandise by location that is potentially a candidate for supply contracts.
- Standards for creating the bids and accepting responses; metrics for evaluation of the responses; process for bid optimization, landed cost calculations, lifecycle costs of the contract, service-level expectations, performance metrics, compliance expectations, and any other constraints that may potentially affect the cost and services.
- Preferred terms for credit, returns, quality, pricing, shipping, insurance, and resolution process for contract-related exceptions.
- Past spend with the suppliers in the bidding process, historical supplier performance and scorecards. These inputs can help in creating a favorable negotiation environment for the buyer.
- Timelines for establishing sources of supply.

The process outputs are typically:

- Established supply contracts
- Ability to leverage them, track them, and manage them through their active life

RELATED SUBPROCESSES

Bid Optimization   When the historic and projected demands, demand origin, demand patterns, and landed costs are known for the merchandise under consideration, then the bid optimization process can help analyze the bids to provide the most optimal proposal. These processes use mathematical modeling to minimize the total costs during the projected lifetime of the contract given the demand forecast. While these processes can provide substantial savings, they require large amounts of data with a high level of confidence in data accuracy.

Purchase Optimization   The purchase optimization process helps in creating a purchase plan and executing the purchases by considering projected demand, and computing cost of fulfillment with the available contracts/sources of supply. The process for optimizing the purchases is similar to bid optimization, with one major difference: This process considers individual time buckets for planning, whereas the bid optimizers usually simply treat the whole contract term as a single time bucket. Purchase optimization processes produce a purchase plan that computes the lowest fulfillment cost plan for the material needs, specifying contracts against which the purchase orders should be created. As the process considers the contract constraints, the purchase plans have the added benefit of being compliant with all supply contracts and can save potential penalties.

Purchase optimization can also be part of the replenishment planning covered earlier as part of the planning functions.

Global Spend Analysis   Spend analysis aids in understanding the total spend with a supplier across all products and divisions of the company. A global understanding of the total spend can enhance buyers' negotiating power with a supplier, and encourages the two parties to appreciate the mutually beneficial relationship.

However, for larger corporations with many divisions, one of the challenges for such analysis is inconsistency of master data. Business units within a large enterprise routinely have common items and vendors, but inconsistent systems and data management tools that prevent them from reconciling and leveraging such information assets.

Therefore, any enterprise-level consolidation and analysis like global spend analysis generally requires highly evolved business intelligence infrastructure along with a good master data management system.

Global Supplier Scorecard   Supplier scorecards can reflect supplier performance on many different metrics. Examples of such metrics are fulfillment rates, lead-time, quality, returns, cost and cost trends, process compliance, technology compliance, and service-level compliance. These metrics are created from very granular transactions that include every purchase interaction with the supplier. Some of these metrics can be consolidated into a global scorecard that is common to all suppliers and provides a consistent measuring tool, and can be helpful in prioritizing the suppliers during processes such as the bid evaluations.

The supplier performance management process is covered in detail under its own section; global scorecarding is simply a byproduct of the process that can be leveraged to effectively manage supplier performance.

Supply Contract Management   Establishing long-term supply contracts is a popular way to establish stability around merchandise and raw material supplies and costs. However, corporations need to manage the contracts to leverage the negotiated terms and prices, enhance the partner relationship, and proactively manage contract lifecycles.

Supply contracts have effective dates. When the contract expires, it must be reevaluated and renewed based on current needs. Contract management applications provide some of the functionality required for managing supply contracts, though most such commercially available solutions lack any serious depth of features in this area. Generally, contract management requires the following functions:

- *Document management.* All contracts need to be managed through an effective *document management system.* Preferably, the contracts should be digitized with the ability to search and retrieve them using flexible user-configured options based on data such as supplier, products, dates, and so on. Digital persistence of contracts makes it easier to archive and to retrieve data efficiently when needed.

- *Proactive leverage and compliance.* Contracts should also be modeled through a flexible data model so that they can be effectively leveraged for best pricing, rebates, and discounts that have been negotiated with the suppliers. The purchase orders can then be tracked against the contracts and effective prices/invoices validated against the negotiated price tiers.

- *Renewal alerts.* When the contracts are about to expire, proactive alerts can be generated for the intended user/buyer community, who can start the action required to renew, cancel, or discontinue the contract in place. This may involve evaluating the projected demand of the products, changed supply situation, currency variations, assortment changes, and any number of factors that affect the retailer's planned intentions. The buyer will also decide whether a new bid should be tendered, or whether simply renegotiating with the existing supplier should suffice. Such proactive alerts on contract status save valuable time by triggering the evaluation and negotiation process promptly.

- *Purchase cost optimization.* Where long-term contracts exist with multiple suppliers and/or shipping locations, the demand forecast can be used to optimize the purchase plans using mathematical modeling. Such optimization will ensure that all purchases comply with contract terms while also minimizing the total current and projected cost of purchases. Though not very common, such solutions not only provide real cost savings, but also prevent contract disputes by modeling the contract terms as real constraints in the planning process.

- *Contract compliance and exception resolution.* An equally important part of managing contracts is managing the exceptions when contract violations occur, or when compliance with contract terms is less than satisfactory. These situations may involve noncompliance with the service-level agreement (SLA), or the process, or pricing and quantity disputes. This requires that supplier performance is tracked against the expected agreed standards in the contract for service levels and process, and that invoices and orders are tracked for agreed prices and quantity obligations.

Most retailers have simple reporting solutions that provide the inputs required to resolve disputed issues.

Companies that spend a substantial amount of their purchase budgets through supply contracts should seriously consider automating their bidding, evaluation, award, and contract management processes. Automation provides opportunity for efficiency gains, as well as additional savings by enhancing the buyer's ability to track contract status and leverage the consolidated buying power of the corporation.

Replenishment Execution

This process refers to the process of creating and executing fulfillment orders to address demand. The process starts when replenishment planning creates distribution orders, work orders, or purchase order suggestions. All of these order types eventually fulfill one or another type of demand when they are executed.

Distribution orders are typically created when the replenishment planning determines that the demand can be optimally fulfilled from the warehouses or other internal stocking locations, and merely requires merchandise to be moved from one internal location to another. The replenishment execution process then manages the lifecycle of the distribution orders, fulfilling the demand that triggered the process. The distribution orders may require authorization or approval before they are sent to the warehouse for inventory allocation and shipping.

Work orders are created when the demand to be addressed must be fulfilled through a manufacturing facility. These work orders are released to the factories, which are directed to manufacture products required to fulfill the demand.

The purchase order suggestions are created when the replenishment planning determines that the best way to fulfill the demand is through vendors. The replenishment execution process takes the purchase order suggestions, converts them into purchase orders, and manages these orders through their lifecycle of approval, transmission to supplier, fulfillment, receipt, and settlement.

The replenishment execution process helps in managing the operations and transactional flow to fulfill the demand at the warehouses, factories, and stores by answering the following questions:

- What purchase suggestions are outstanding? What replenishment exceptions exist that require a user review or approval? Which replenishment proposals are ready to be converted into firm orders?
- What orders are currently scheduled for delivery at the warehouse, or the factory, or the store on a given day?
- Where do these orders originate from?
- What products and quantities are on order? Which orders have been confirmed for fulfillment? Which orders have been backordered?
- Which orders are late and need to be expedited? Which orders are at risk of becoming late where acknowledgments or advanced shipping notices (ASNs) are expected but not received?
- What is the status of the inventories, on-hand, expected receipts, and expected shipments at any warehouse location? What is the projected stockout risk?

Demand fulfillment at stores can be executed through internal transfers from a warehouse, or with direct shipments to the stores from suppliers' warehouses. Warehouses are typically replenished through purchase orders that are fulfilled by external vendors or manufacturers. All the transaction mechanisms mentioned here help execute the demand fulfillment function from both internal and external sources of supply. The following sections provide descriptions of distribution orders, work orders, and purchase orders.

Distribution or Transfer Orders

These orders are generated when merchandise is required to be transferred from one *internal* facility to another. These transfers cover the movement of merchandise from warehouse to store, warehouse to factory, factory to warehouse, warehouse to warehouse, and store to store.

The majority of the transfers for retailers fall in the first category, which moves merchandise from warehouses to stores. However, retailers use interwarehouse and interstore transfers frequently when such inventory redistribution makes sense, or for immediate order fulfillment or when the shipping optimization may dictate such indirect movements. The transfers between warehouse and factory generally reflect manufacturing material requests for raw materials from the factory, or the movement of finished goods from factory to warehouse.

It is worth remembering that the cost of transfer of material is typically not a consideration for distribution orders as most corporations use standard costing as the basis for inventory valuation of such transfers.

Distribution orders are created by the replenishment system, and are approved by the user/system as configured. These are then integrated into the warehouse management applications for acknowledgment, execution, confirmation, and inventory reconciliation. On fulfilling the distribution order, the warehouses generate an advanced shipping notice (ASN) for the destination facility and send inventory reconciliation back to the replenishment planning and ERP systems.

Exhibit 6.1 shows purchase orders and transfer orders in the retail context.

Work Orders

Work orders are typically used to direct the manufacturing processes. Consider a make-to-order manufacturing environment where work orders are created in response to customer orders; in this case, they also help in tracking the customer order status throughout the manufacturing process. Alternatively, in make-to-stock situations, work orders can simply be an

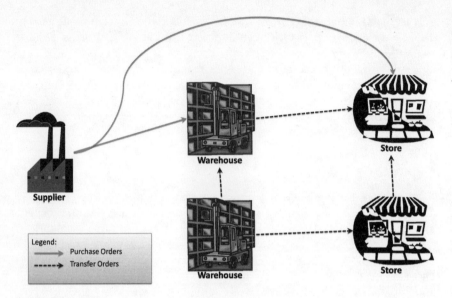

EXHIBIT 6.1 Purchase Orders and Transfer Orders

output of the production planning process, and act as a mechanism to control and direct factory production operations. Work orders can be created for products as well as services.

Work orders provide the mechanism for factories to schedule manufacturing operations and resources and consume raw materials. As work orders relate the demand to the manufacturing activity, they provide a reconciliation mechanism for accounting for the costs of this manufacturing activity. The manufacturing costs in this situation become part of the cost of goods sold.

Purchase Orders

Purchase orders are generated using the proposed order quantities from the replenishment system when the demand needs to be fulfilled from external suppliers. The purchase orders may go through a formal *approval workflow* before being confirmed. The approval workflow for purchasing may be very simple and automated, where the system validates a few rules and automatically approves the requisitions or orders. For example, all purchase orders that are below $1,000 may be approved by the system, after validating that these purchase orders are being raised on the approved vendors and have correct contract references for the ordered items. Alternatively, they may involve manual approval steps when certain conditions are met, such as the value of the order, or the supplier on which the order is being placed, or the receiving location. Continuing the example, if the contract references on an order were invalid, then the system might present this order for manual approval before it is released. The approval workflows are supported with flexible technology solutions that use sophisticated rules engines, event definitions, alerts, and actions. Users can then define their own approval workflow steps, which typically change from one company to another.

Purchasing through long-term supply contracts provides another opportunity to optimize the source of supplies by leveraging the contract pricing, contract status, and other cost parameters that affect the total landed cost. If future projected demand is available, that can also be considered to determine the optimal purchase orders plans over the whole planning horizon. Such optimization helps in reducing total purchase costs over the planning horizon, while simultaneously enhancing demand fulfillment rates.

Once the approved purchase orders are created, they are transmitted to the suppliers for fulfillment.

Depending on the process and the SLA between the supplier and the enterprise, the purchase order lifecycle can go through several stages, such as acknowledgment, changes to original quantity and delivery schedules, ready-to-ship notices, ASN, shipment, receipts, and final settlement. Most of these states of a purchase order are confirmed using industry-standard formats, the most popular being the X12 standards for electronic data exchange (EDI) transactions. The Accredited Standards Committee (ASC) X12 was chartered by the American National Standards Institute (ANSI) to develop uniform standards for interindustry electronic exchange of business transactions, now popularly known as the *EDI standards*.

The *purchase order (PO)* is the initial document that consists of the merchandise, quantity, costs, taxes, need dates, and delivery location information with supplier, contract reference, and other terms and conditions. EDI 850 represents the purchase order.

A *purchase order acknowledgment* may be sent back from the supplier to acknowledge and confirm the quantities to be fulfilled. When this is required, it is also normally subject to a process SLA so that suppliers are obliged to send back this confirmation within a given time period. Suppliers may be allowed to change the quantities and/or delivery schedules at this point, depending on their contract terms with the enterprise. Not all companies use PO acknowledgments, though it can help reduce the variability in their procurement process through fulfillment schedules that are confirmed by the supplier. These are typically more reliable than the expected or required PO delivery schedules. Purchase order acknowledgments are exchanged through the EDI 855 transaction set.

Once the supplier is ready to ship the purchase orders, suppliers are required to determine the approved shipping method. When the cost of shipping is included in the price of goods (e.g., when the quoted cost basis is ex-destination), the supplier is responsible for shipping the goods.

However, when the cost of shipping is not included in the price, the retailers typically provide guidelines for the suppliers to follow. In this case, there are a couple of possibilities:

- If the supplier is responsible for shipping, then suppliers follow a document called a *routing guide* that is published by most large retailers. This guide lays down the process of selecting the shipper based on the lanes/routes. Retailers routinely verify the shipping compliance with the routing guide before paying for the shipments.
- If the buyer company is responsible for shipping, then the suppliers send out the *request for routing* document to the buyer. This may be an automated EDI request, or a *ready-to-ship* event created through the Web portal. This document contains information on items, shipping origin, quantities, weights, volumes, and transportation classification of the current shipment. The buyer company then uses this information to create loads and plan routes; it tenders the loads to carriers, and after the tender has been accepted, it returns a *routing instructions* document back to the supplier. This document tells the supplier who is the carrier and when to expect the merchandise pickup.

When the merchandise on the purchase order is received, the financial settlement process starts. For internal distribution orders, it simply means a transfer on the corporate books for the inventory shipped from the warehouse to the store or another location. For external purchase orders on a supplier, the settlement process consists of receiving an invoice from the supplier, verifying the invoice, and paying for the goods/services supplied.

When an invoice from a supplier is received, the verification and approval process may use a *three-way match*. This is shown in Exhibit 6.2. The process is called a three-way match because it consists of validating the invoice against the purchase order and shipment/receipt details. This is a relatively standard validation procedure and is supported by most of the enterprise applications supporting purchase order management and accounts payable.

Inputs and Outputs of the Replenishment Execution Process

The replenishment execution process manages the lifecycle of the distribution orders, work orders, and the purchase orders. It needs the following inputs:

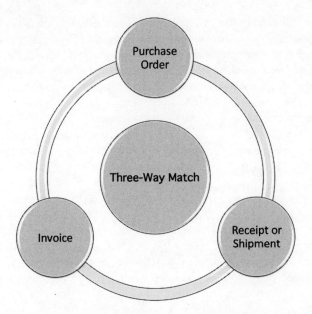

EXHIBIT 6.2 Three-Way Match for Merchandise Invoice Verification

- Suggested order quantities, fulfillment methods, and other order parameters for creating and managing the purchase orders, work orders, and distribution orders.
- Approval workflows for creating and executing the above orders. Approvals are routinely required for executing the purchase orders, and in some cases before executing work orders and distribution orders as well.

As the process takes the distribution orders, work orders, and purchase orders through their lifecycles, it manages their status, produces reports, alerts, and exceptions, and helps in resolving any issues before closing the transaction. This can be considered as the output of this function.

Production Scheduling

The production scheduling process works within the constraints defined by the production planning process to create manufacturing schedules for the shop-floor. With the advanced planning systems prevalent in production planning and scheduling, the execution schedules can be seen as a continuous spectrum of the planning process where every process iteration models the manufacturing resources to a more granular level and produces a plan that is closer to an execution schedule.

The main difference between the production planning and scheduling processes is that the latter must enforce production sequencing and must model shop-floor resources to create feasible manufacturing schedules. The abstraction and aggregate representation of resources that is possible in the planning process is no more desirable in the scheduling processes that need modeling of individual resources. Exact production routing, with specific resources, setup time, processing time, and labor and operator skills required, must be modeled for producing feasible shop-floor schedules.

Both the production planning and the scheduling processes are too large in their functional scope and modeling parameters to be covered with any completeness in this book. However, as both of these are integral parts of a manufacturing supply chain, the intent is to cover the basic concepts and their place in the overall supply chain.

Production planning and scheduling processes also support product availability and promising functions. *Available to promise (ATP)* checks can quickly determine whether a specific order can be fulfilled from the inventory in the supply chain. Such inventory can either be on-hand inventory or based on projected receipts from supply processes like manufacturing or purchase. A more intensive promising mechanism, *capable to promise (CTP)*, not only checks the existing and projected inventories but also considers the available manufacturing capacity and materials to create promises based on manufacturing activity scheduled for the future. Both of these availability checks help in creating promises for order fulfillment, which are based on feasible operational plans and are appropriately constrained by the material and capacity limitations.

The production planning process produces a daily schedule of operations with production targets, resource availability, and material availability. The production scheduling typically takes these parameters as inputs and models individual labor, assets, material, and routing to produce the hourly schedule of operation for the shop-floor.

It typically addresses the following questions:

- Schedule of operations for a specific factory floor, showing labor and machine-level scheduling, material required, setup changes, production-run quantities, and start-time and end-time for each individual production operation and workstation.
- Material required for the day's production. This can be either pulled from factory stores, as is done in discrete manufacturing, or backflushed for reconciliation, as in the case of process-based manufacturing.
- Asset, material, and resource utilization for the day.

Inputs and Outputs of the Production Scheduling Process

To produce the daily operation plan for the factory, the production scheduling process requires the following inputs:

- Production routing for the scheduled operations. Production routing typically shows the sequence of operations to be carried out to produce a specific product or subassembly. For each operation, it has further details on setup required, time required, workstation or machining center where it is done, operator requirements, required materials, required tools and equipment, inspection procedure, and specific skills needed to complete the operation.
- Target production for the day by product or subassembly.
- Calendars showing availability of all resources, including workstations, operators, equipment, and tools.
- Raw material and subassemblies availability.

The scheduling process generally utilizes heuristics (rules) to create a feasible operation schedule for the day for the factory floor. The process may utilize forward scheduling, backward scheduling, or a combination of the two to allocate resources and plan operations. Most often, the objective of this process is to reduce the number of production changeovers, to reduce the setup time associated with these changes, increase asset utilization, and level labor resource utilization, while simultaneously working within the constraints of the production targets, material, and resource availability.

The output of the process is a feasible operations plan for the factory shop-floor. These plans specify the production schedules, resource schedules, and material schedules on a daily basis for each manufacturing facility.

Supplier Performance Management

Supplier performance management processes have gained importance as the dependence on suppliers for reliable execution has increased. Fulfillment rates have been conventionally measured for suppliers, but more recently process compliance and service-level compliance have become standard metrics for supplier scorecarding. The wide adoption of electronic communications has been a major driving force behind this change as it provides accurate and reliable data for compliance and performance measurements. In some cases, *value-added network (VAN)* providers that support the electronic communications also host the supplier compliance applications that make it easier to adopt this process quickly. Therefore, once a corporation on-boards its critical partners to use automated electronic communications extensively, and establishes partnership with a VAN provider, deploying supplier performance measurement metrics is not only the next logical step, but can be facilitated by some VAN providers.

Suppliers (in a generic sense, this includes merchandise suppliers and carriers alike) play a huge role in the smooth operations of a retailer, especially in the execution phase. They affect what gets shipped, where, how much, when, and in some cases, how. Retailers need to maintain their service levels to make sure that their shelves are adequately stocked with the right merchandise. This is not a small job, given the large assortments, complex replenishment processes, and large number of suppliers with the ability to affect the services that a retailer must depend on. Similar requirements exist in other industry verticals, and the ability to measure supplier effectiveness provides control to managers to run their operations smoothly.

Supplier performance measurement processes answer the following questions:

- What are the fulfillment rate metrics for suppliers and products?
- Are the suppliers following the process guidelines of the enterprise? Are the processes successfully automated? Are there any manual touchpoints that make the process inefficient? Are there opportunities to automate the interaction? What kind of data issues exist that may hinder such automation?
- Are suppliers keeping their SLAs?
- Who are the best and worst suppliers? Where should collaboration priorities and dollars be focused?

Most large corporations measure their suppliers for good execution performance and process compliance. The metrics for measuring supplier performance can be divided into two categories, as discussed in the following.

Fulfillment Execution Metrics

Fulfillment execution measures how effectively suppliers fulfill the orders for material. These metrics revolve around three main factors—quantity, quality, and time—as shown in Exhibit 6.3.

1. *Quantity.* This metric provides the fulfillment rates. There are various quantities that could be measured for effectively measuring the order fulfillment process. These are Ordered versus Confirmed; Confirmed versus Shipped; Shipped versus Received; Shipped versus Invoiced; and finally a fill-rate calculation that makes sense for the corporation. The most relevant *fill-rate* definition is to compare Ordered Quantity to Received Quantity. Other quantity comparisons mentioned above,

EXHIBIT 6.3 Supplier Fulfillment Performance Measurement

if routinely short of expectations, simply point to the subprocess that may be underoptimized and needs attention. For example, a persistent inconsistency between the shipped and received quantities should point to pilferage, packaging issues, or even equipment issues.

A *perfect order* metric is usually a composite metric generated from the above as orders that were fulfilled on time, complete, damage-free, and accurately invoiced. However, there is no single definition of *perfect order*; this metric can be computed based on what is most relevant to know for the buyer corporation.

2. *Quality.* Most retailers do not require inspection on inbound merchandise, though that may be a prevalent practice with the manufacturers. However, the quality of received materials matters to all. In a manufacturing environment, poor quality will result in wastage of labor and material when the finished goods do not pass the quality tests. The later in the manufacturing process the defect is found, the higher is the wastage in terms of labor and material. For manufacturers, quality control for received materials is an extensive process using statistical quality control (SQC), which also provides the incoming quality compliance reports on the suppliers.

For retailers, poor-quality merchandise affects their operations through increased consumer returns, unsatisfied customers, and additional labor to process returns. Retailers can get a good grasp on quality by measuring Damaged Packages, Damaged Goods, and Customer

Returns. The first two can be made part of the warehouse SOP (standard operating procedure). Damaged packages can be recorded on receipt by visually checking and flagging the transaction. Damaged goods are recorded when pallets are broken into cases/boxes/eaches for fulfilling an outbound shipment from the warehouse. Customer returns are typically captured through the store-returns process for stores and return merchandise authorization (RMA) transactions for other channels like Web storefronts, mail catalogs, and call center orders.

3. *Time.* Within this third metric for measuring the effectiveness of the fulfillment process, there are two types of time metrics that can be tracked:

1. *Lead-time.* There are various types of lead-times that are important. The total fulfillment lead-time consists of lead-time components that are controlled together by the supplier and the carrier. Some of these components are the Order Acknowledgment Lead-Time, defined as the time between the order (EDI 850) transmission date and order acknowledgment (EDI 855) receipt; Order Processing Lead-Time, defined as the time between order (EDI 850) transmission date and ready-to-ship (RTS) message (typically EDI document 753, also called *request for routing*); Ready-to-Ship Confirmation Lead-Time, defined as the time between receiving an EDI 753 request and sending back an EDI 754 (routing instructions document); and finally Transportation Transit Lead-Time, defined as the time between pickup shipment status message (EDI 214) and yard-check-in time at the destination facility. Keeping tabs at the lead-time provides realistic data for replenishment systems that helps create correct demand forecasts. Trends in lead-time usually point to a broken subprocess. Unstable lead-times will result in supply volatility, which makes the planning process harder and almost always results in higher inventory levels to maintain stable service levels to downstream facilities.

2. *Activity-level service-level agreement (SLA).* These SLAs control the on-time execution of key activities in the fulfillment process. For example, the buyer may require the suppliers to send PO acknowledgements within 48 hours of PO transmission. The buyer may use these acknowledgements to reconcile their supply plans especially when the supplier is unable to confirm the PO quantities as requested. These violations do not necessarily create supply volatility, but can cause localized disruptions of schedules, higher cost of operations, and morale issues. For example, if a carrier routinely violates the pickup and delivery-time windows, then the warehouse and store managers have to manage schedule disruptions, potentially pay overtime to staff, and/or make last-minute changes to labor scheduling.

Once these metrics are measured, they can be shared with the suppliers as a *scorecard*. Enterprises can use these scorecards to identify their best and worst suppliers and prioritize their spend and relationships. Some enterprises also use chargebacks when suppliers fail to live up to contracted service levels.

Process Compliance Metrics

Well-established processes normally provide repeatable performance that is efficient, highly automated, and does not depend on an individual associate's skills to achieve a dependable result. Purchasing processes cross organizational boundaries and their total efficacy depends on how well suppliers comply with the retailer's processes. Measuring process compliance helps an enterprise identify the suppliers with issues, and address these issues before they start affecting supply chain efficiency.

The key to a successful process compliance program is to identify which transactions are core to the smooth functioning of the purchasing and delivery processes. Then, for the targeted transactions, the key data elements belonging to these transactions need to be clearly identified. Finally, expectations should be plainly defined, and should be adopted in the contracts with the partner so that both parties clearly understand them.

Such transactions for process compliance can cover the merchandise suppliers as well as carriers, and can consist of all the following:

- Purchase order acknowledgment, request for routing instructions, advanced shipping notice, and merchandise invoices for the suppliers
- Load tender request and response, shipment status message, and freight invoices for the carriers

Automating these transactions, for example, through EDI messages, helps in preempting situations where the process is about to break down, and in prompt resolution of an undesirable situation.

Process compliance metrics normally measure the following three aspects of any transaction, which are shown in Exhibit 6.4:

1. *Service-level agreement (SLA) compliance.* This measures whether a required transaction response was sent within the agreed time. For example, if PO acknowledgments are expected for every PO within 24 hours of transmission, then this metric will track how many POs did not get any acknowledgments, and how many acknowledgments were received after the required 24 hours SLA. This SLA metric can be applied to all the transactions mentioned earlier. Buyers should decide to measure specific transaction SLA compliance only if it helps them

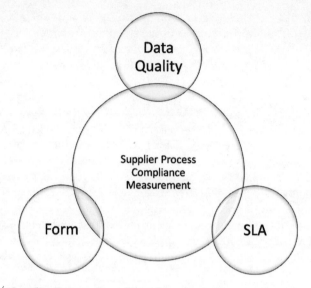

EXHIBIT 6.4 Supplier Process Compliance Measurement

identify process inefficiencies, or when such an SLA is part of a contractual agreement between the buyer and the supplier.

For example, if PO acknowledgments are used to project on-order quantities and enable order promising, it will be a good transaction to track. However, if no other functionality depends on this transaction, then there is no need to track this SLA.

2. *Format compliance.* This measures whether the required transaction had any format issues that may have caused the transaction communication to fail. Most business transactions these days are exchanged using standard industry formats automatically between the buyer and supplier computer systems. For the computer systems to recognize a given transaction, it must follow a predefined format. This ensures that the automation does not fail and transactions are not dropped unexpectedly through the process due to formatting errors. Every automated transaction that requires a manual touch adds to the cost of operations. For example, for the process between the two computer systems to work smoothly, it may be required that the dates are transmitted in mmddyyyy format. For EDI formats, such formatting requirements can be quite stringent for the required segments and the data elements within.

This metric measures the number of transactions that are rejected by the buyer's systems due to such format errors. Therefore, it becomes most relevant for electronic transaction exchange (EDI/XML/preformatted files).

3. *Content quality compliance.* This metric is designed to measure the data quality of the transactions exchanged. For example, assume that an ASN must reference the PO number, and that the retailer's applications depend on matching this PO number with a valid purchase order number in the system, before allowing a shipment to be received in the warehouse. Now every ASN where such information is missing needs to be manually received and reconciled, adding to the cost of receiving. In this situation, having a metric that will measure the number of ASNs that did not have the PO number (the field was left blank), and number of ASNs that had an invalid PO reference (the field was populated with an invalid PO number) will be most reasonable. This data can be shared with the vendor to review the process and to ensure that such errors are reduced over time to within acceptable limits. Of course, this means that such "required" fields are clearly identified and communicated to the partners in advance.

As with the fulfillment execution metrics, these metrics can be shared with the suppliers as a *scorecard*. If noncompliance is a big concern, this scorecard can prioritize the efforts of the compliance teams on the partners at the bottom of the compliance reporting. If contract terms allow, retailers can charge back the extra costs due to noncompliant processes to their suppliers, and create a financial incentive for vendors to comply with the process.

Inputs and Outputs for Measuring the Supplier Performance

For measuring the fulfillment metrics, the following inputs are required:

- Purchase orders, purchase order acknowledgments, requests for routing instructions, advanced shipping notices, merchandise receipt transactions, and merchandise invoices
- Load tender request and response, shipment status message, freight invoices, proof of delivery, yard check in, and yard check out
- Damage-in-transit and damaged-goods receipt transactions
- Lifecycle events data on the above transactions
- Contractual service-level agreement definitions to determine what transactions are covered and to identify exceptions when they occur

The data is compiled, processed, related, and reported to produce the above metrics that cover the quantity, quality, and time (SLA) compliance for the supplies. These metrics and scorecards are the output of the process.

Global Trade Management

Global trade management processes cover imports, exports, financial services, and declarations management. An overview of these processes is presented in this section.

Global trade management primarily addresses the following questions:

- Do enterprise imports and exports follow country-specific regulations and comply with the prohibited items and vendors lists?
- Is the enterprise able to leverage the preferential trade agreements to save on customs and other duties?
- Are the import and export duties and taxes appropriately calculated, and do they pose any compliance risk?
- What are the best methods for financing and settling the imports?
- Are the items involved in global trade properly classified for duty and tax calculations?

Imports and Exports Management

Most countries have laws governing exports and imports. They also have taxes, duties, and other surcharges controlling such cross-border trade. Therefore, any corporation dealing with exports and imports needs to be aware of these governance structures, and must comply with them to legally conduct their business.

The actual transactions and processes that support such trade may also vary for exports and imports. For example, an import purchase order may go through an iterative process with the supplier for acknowledgment and acceptance to supply the ordered quantities on time, before becoming a binding contract. Similarly, the financing of import orders, especially from the Far East, may involve prepayments, credit letters, guarantees, and other financial instruments that are generally not seen in domestic trade.

The specific processes for exports and imports will vary greatly from country to country, and therefore it is not possible to cover all these functions in detail along with all their variations. Therefore, the following sections provide a general overview of common governance structures involved in managing global trade processes.

The following concepts should be helpful to understand the functional scope of imports and exports processes.

CLASSIFICATION   Most countries use some kind of classification system to group the merchandise flowing through their borders. These classes are published and used for calculating the export and import tariff due to be paid during trade. In the United States, the harmonized tariff system (HTS) and export control classification number (ECCN) are two examples of such product classification data.

While customs will assess the duties to be paid for every such transaction, it may be a time-consuming process. An alternative for larger corporations is to estimate the duties and make such payments, pending reconciliation and final settlement. Most corporations in the United States can register as an importer or exporter with the customs bureau and establish "preferred" status based on trade volumes, past history of assessments and settlements, and other criteria. With preferred status, corporations can provide the details of trade through specific customs documentation and self-assess the tariff. U.S. customs can then decide to let the shipments pass or audit them. This saves considerable time on the docks, enhancing supply chain flow efficiencies and lowering the overall costs of imports/exports.

The classification data is published by customs, and is also available from third-party data providers as electronic feeds for the systems used by the customs brokers or corporations to assess their tariffs.

COMPLIANCE AND PREFERENTIAL TRADE   Exports and imports are also subject to federal policies and rules compliance. Some goods and services are restricted from imports and exports and lists of these are regularly published and updated. It is the responsibility of the corporations to ensure compliance with these lists.

Similarly, trade is not allowed with all parties or countries. A blacklist for sanctioned parties/embargo lists are used to publish and control trade with blacklisted countries, corporations, and individuals.

Preferential trade agreements allow corporations to take advantage of special trade zones, such as NAFTA (North American Free Trade Association). As importers, buyers need to maintain vendor declarations for taking advantage of such preferential trade arrangements. The vendor declarations certify the origin of goods and are required to qualify goods for preferred rates of duty. As exporters, companies may have to issue a similar certificate of origin to their customers. Preferential trade requires determination of eligibility of products for preferential treatment and may depend on clearly defining the origin, especially when the products are manufactured across multiple locations.

Finally, an enterprise must have export and import licenses for cross-border trading. Enterprises must allocate licenses for selected products and also determine whether a license is required for a particular transaction.

CUSTOMS SERVICES   Customs services for imports and exports consist of creating and exchanging the correct sets of documents with the customs agencies. In some countries, this documentation has been standardized and can be exchanged electronically. However, paper-based documentation is still widely in use. These documents include the export or import declarations, bills of lading, invoicing, duty assessment, exit/entry summaries, and so on.

FINANCIAL SERVICES   Financial services cover the financing and settlement processes for the imports and exports. Some of the terms, processes, and descriptions that are common in imports and exports are discussed here.

Buyers can use *unsecured open account* terms to make payments at a specific date in the future. With an unsecured account, the buyer does not have to establish a negotiable instrument with the bank or a financial institute acting as an intermediary. Ownership of the merchandise typically changes hands *prior* to the payment. These are highly favorable terms for the buyer. This type of arrangement can be set up by buyers with strong credit history, or where the seller trusts the buyer and a long-term relationship exists between the two companies.

Another common method for international trade is *documentary collections*. This involves payments through a bank acting as an intermediary. The bank settles the transaction by *exchanging documents*, causing a simultaneous payment and transfer of ownership. This protects both the parties as the buyer does not have to pay in advance and the seller retains the ownership until the payment is made.

A *letter of credit* is the most widely used method for international trade settlement. It is a formal letter issued to the buyer's bank that authorizes the seller to draw drafts on the bank under specified conditions. These conditions are negotiated between the buyer and seller, and usually are based on events like quality inspection clearance, delivery on dock, and so on. As above, the bank acts as an intermediary and deals only with the documents and not the merchandise.

There are various types of letters of credit in use. A *revocable letter of credit* can be amended or even canceled unilaterally by the buyer, and can be very unfavorable to the seller. An *irrevocable letter of credit* cannot be amended or canceled without the common consent of the buyer and seller. A *confirmed letter of credit* is guaranteed by another bank of established credit that guarantees the payment if the original bank issuing the letter fails to do so. An *unconfirmed letter of credit* does not carry any guarantees from another bank. A *sight letter of credit* is payable when documents are presented in compliance with the original terms and conditions, whereas a *time draft letter of credit* becomes payable at a predetermined time in the future given the documents are presented in good order.

Letters of credit can be used not only for payments for purchases, but also to finance the manufacturer/exporter. This involves a deferred payment structure where the payments to the manufacturer/exporter are executed at predetermined future dates. These may be linked to predetermined events such as start of manufacturing, clearing of the inspection, loading onto the ship, and so on.

Inputs and Outputs of the Global Trade Management Process

Global trade management is a process with a wide scope and specialized needs. It is hard to present any comprehensive list of inputs and outputs for this process, though the following list should be a good starting point:

- Master data for items, vendors, certificates of origin, service providers for drayage, customs, and carrier services
- Item classification for customs duties, screened parties lists, certificate-of-origin details, prohibited lists for imports and exports
- Data on preferential trade agreements, customs duties
- Financial services providers, credit limits, preferred instruments for financing imports, and so on
- Order and shipping documents, bill of lading, and ocean schedules

The process primarily ensures compliance with various country-specific regulations, establishes the duties to be paid, helps in clearing goods for imports and exports, manages financial settlements for global trade, and so on. The main outputs from the global trade management process can be:

- Customs documentation for all import and export transactions, import and export clearances
- Duty calculations for imports, product classifications, trade agreement references, certificates of origin
- Letters of credit and other financial instruments used for settlement

Summary

Supply management processes relate to a large scope of supply chain functions that help in fulfilling the demand. Because demand can be fulfilled from internal or external sources, the mechanisms to execute the fulfillment process vary from purchase orders, to transfer orders, to work orders.

Demand can be fulfilled from external sources such as vendors, using purchase orders. The purchasing process is supported by other functions such as sourcing, vendor selection, and contract management. Sourcing and vendor selection helps companies in establishing a standard process to identify vendors, evaluate the potential relationship, on-board these as partners in the purchase process, and track and manage their performance on a continuous basis. Contract management processes cover the bidding, bid evaluation, contract award, and contract tracking functions. Supply contracts help in reducing supply and price volatility and are generally established for critical raw materials, seasonal merchandise, and exclusively branded merchandise.

When demand is fulfilled from internal sources, the facilitating transaction is called a transfer order when required material is available in a warehouse. If the required goods need to be manufactured in a factory, a work order is generally used to drive such production. The production scheduling process then takes over to schedule the manufacturing operations to meet such demand. Production scheduling processes typically use sequencing techniques, and consider material and resource constraints to ensure that these schedules can be executed as planned.

Supply management also provides the processes for managing vendor relationships and tracks their performance. Vendor performance may be measured for fulfillment rates, on-time shipments, quality, and cost aspects.

When purchases involve international vendors, global trade management functions support the special aspects of these transactions. Some of the additional issues for imports or exports are material classification and restrictions for import/export, customs duties, value added tax (VAT), financing, trade agreements, and screened-party management.

CHAPTER 7

Transportation Management

Material distribution is a core supply chain function in most business operations. In the manufacturing industry, it is the movement of raw materials from the vendors' warehouses to factories, and of the finished goods from the factories to the distribution warehouses. In retail, such movements extend from vendors to the retailer's warehouses, and then to the stores. As a large retailer can have thousands of stores, supported by a large number of warehouses, the efficiency of the distribution of merchandise from warehouses to stores is very important and can have a substantial impact on profitability.

Transportation management functions address these business needs to move goods and merchandise from one location to another, pay for such moves, buy the required shipping capacity, track the movements of material in transit, and manage the transportation assets if they were owned by the retailer.

The two other functions that would also be within the scope of transportation management are covered in Chapter 5. These are the transportation procurement and transportation capacity planning functions. These two functions are less frequent, and are expected to be completed prior to any of the transportation management functions in supply chain execution.

Transportation Planning and Execution

The transportation planning and execution processes help in optimally moving the merchandise from one location to another. Any business process that needs merchandise movements from one point to another can be optimized by using the transportation planning functions. These movements can be between two internal locations, such as shipping from warehouses to the stores, or between an external location such as a supplier's warehouse and an internal location like one of the retailer's warehouses or stores.

Recall from the replenishment execution discussions in Chapter 6 that purchase orders, work orders, and distribution orders are used as transaction mechanisms to manage material movements. The transportation optimization process leverages all these transactions to plan for the best method of moving the merchandise from one location to another.

The transportation planning process primarily consists of reviewing all the purchase orders or internal fulfillment orders that are ready to ship. The orders are typically flagged as "ready to ship" when the inventory to fulfill these orders has been identified and committed. This ready-to-ship trigger can be internal or external to the enterprise. For the purchase orders, this inventory belongs to the supplier, and therefore the supplier identifies the purchase orders that are ready to ship. For the internal material transfers, the same could be done at a warehouse either by a warehouse management system or by an enterprise order fulfillment process that identifies the inventory and allocates it to fulfill such requests.

The transportation planning process then takes all the ready-to-ship orders, and consolidates them based on common source–destination pairs that have the same need dates. Need date is defined as the date when the merchandise is required to reach the destination. Other relevant factors may also be considered during the consolidation process, such as transportation classification of the material to be moved, hazmat flag, special handling instructions, or special equipment required, such as refrigerated vans. The objective of the consolidation process is to aggregate or split orders to create shipments that optimize the loads and the routes while simultaneously constraining on the need dates for delivery and resource constraints. The consolidation process can produce many different types of shipments, such as truckloads (TLs), less-than-truckloads (LTLs), multistop loads, transshipments, and multimodal shipments. To ensure operations feasibility, all of these shipments are constrained based on the need date at the destination, pickup and delivery time windows at origin and destinations, equipment-type constraints, and the shipping mode constraints.

The consolidation step produces the transportation capacity required to ship all these orders along the identified lanes/routes, and transportation modes. Then the transportation planning process looks at all possible alternatives to move this merchandise. This is also called the *resource* or *carrier selection process*. These alternatives exist when many carriers can be used along the identified routes/lanes with available capacity and equipment types. The solution models the cost equations for these alternatives, and may consider other parameters like carrier performance, preferred providers, volume commitments, and continuous moves (opportunistic and/or planned). It solves the problem of optimizing the cost and schedule of shipments. This intermediate output of the transportation solution looks like planned loads that are ready to be shipped with short-listed carriers for each shipment.

The next step in this process is the tendering of these loads to the carriers. The shortlisted carriers are selected based on user preferences, historical performance, available capacity, required equipment type, costs, lanes, and other relevant criteria. This short list may have the contract carriers as well as general carriers that do not have prenegotiated contracts with the company on selected lanes. The planned shipments are tendered to this short list of carriers for acceptance. Once the carriers accept the load tender, the shipment is released to the selected carriers, suppliers, and receivers (external or internal) of the shipment; the relevant parties can use this information for scheduling labor and operations at the shipping source and destination locations.

Exhibit 7.1 provides a quick overview of the transportation planning and execution process as presented here.

Conceptually, the optimization process has two main steps: (1) consolidating shipments to create optimal loads and routes, and (2) resource selection to select the carrier and the equipment. Advanced transportation solutions can formulate the transportation problem to model and solve both of these steps together.

These shipments have now entered the execution phase and can be tracked until they are delivered. The execution phase tracking of shipments

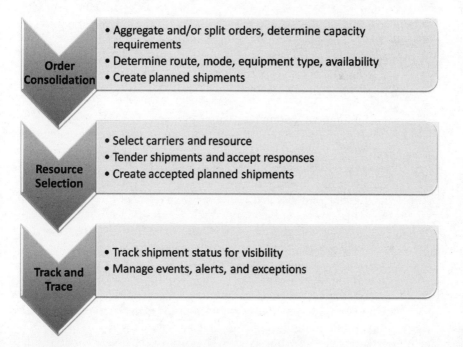

Order Consolidation
- Aggregate and/or split orders, determine capacity requirements
- Determine route, mode, equipment type, availability
- Create planned shipments

Resource Selection
- Select carriers and resource
- Tender shipments and accept responses
- Create accepted planned shipments

Track and Trace
- Track shipment status for visibility
- Manage events, alerts, and exceptions

EXHIBIT 7.1 Transportation Planning and Execution Steps

is usually done using electronic messages between the carrier and the shipper. EDI transaction 214, also called *shipment status message (SSM)*, is used for these messages and it follows an industry-wide standard that is commonly adhered to across all carriers and shippers so that the messages can be interpreted by anyone. In spite of the common definition, partners need to work together for integration testing and successful on-boarding to ensure that their systems can run unattended. Each shipment can generate many such status transactions during its lifetime from pickup to delivery depending on the number of stops.

Other interactions between the shipper and carrier can also use the electronic messages for communications, and such integration makes the process efficient and allows high levels of automation. Examples of such interactions are the load tender that uses EDI transaction 204 and a tender response using EDI 990.

The transportation planning and execution process addresses the following questions:

- What is the most efficient way to move the merchandise for fulfilling the current orders in the supply chain? How should the shipments be built, loads configured, routes selected, and resources and carriers determined?
- What carriers should be selected for managing these moves?
- How much will each shipment cost (estimates based on the carrier contracts)?

The following are some of the relevant industry terms for this process:

Carrier commonly refers to the transportation service provider.
Shipper refers to the entity buying the transportation services from the carrier.
EDI (electronic data interchange) is an industry standard for exchanging electronic messages. More information on types and specific transaction numbers that are commonly used in the supply chain functions is provided in Appendix F.
Ready to ship is a status on an order when the supplier (internal or external) wants to flag an order to be considered for shipment planning. This status also means that the source of the shipment, shipment quantity, and inventory have been identified and committed for this order. This ensures that the correct transportation lane can be picked up, and transportation attributes for the shipment such as weight and volume can be accurately determined.
Consolidation is a subprocess within transportation planning that refers to an initial review of ready-to-ship orders, and creation

of groups that share certain characteristics such as the same source–destination pair and need dates.

Carrier or *resource selection* refers to the subprocess that identifies the shortlisted carriers that are suitable for a planned shipment.

Load is the part of a shipment that will fit on specified equipment (such as an 18-wheeler).

Load tender is the transaction that is used by the shipper to request a shipment pickup or acceptance confirmation from the carrier.

Tender response is the return transaction in response to a load tender that is used by the carrier to accept or reject the shipper's request for a planned shipment pickup.

Track and trace refers to the process of tracking a shipment through its lifecycle as it is picked up from the source and moves through its planned stops to the final destination.

SSMs (shipment status messages) are the messages used for the above track-and-trace process. Each shipment can have several of these messages starting at pickup through multiple stops until the final destination of the shipment.

POD (proof of delivery) is the message that confirms the successful delivery by the carrier at the shipment's destinations. In lieu of the POD, the shipper may consider the final SSM for a planned stop on a shipment's route as the POD for purposes of triggering the subsequent processes.

Continuous moves are the shipment legs that are built to enhance the efficiency of a shipment. It may result in round-trip tours where a carrier picks up merchandise from location A (e.g., a warehouse; see Exhibit 7.2), drops it to a store B, and then goes to the nearest supplier warehouse C to pick up merchandise destined for warehouse A. Continuous moves typically result in higher utilization and lower cost.

Backhaul/deadheading refers to the return leg of a shipment. Deadheading refers to backhauls that are typically empty.

Pool-points/transshipments are shipments that are routed through an intermediate location with the objective of merging them with other shipments to create better loads/efficiencies. This is also called *merge-in-transit*.

Lane/route refers to the transportation lanes between two specified points. A route can consist of multiple lanes. The lanes are typically serviced by a carrier and specified as such in the contracts with the shipper. Each lane has equipment types available and, in some cases, dedicated capacity if desired by the shipper.

Rate is the cost of transportation along a specified lane for a specified equipment type and load type. Transportation planning systems

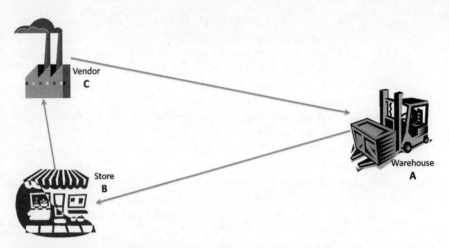

EXHIBIT 7.2 Example of a Continuous Move

use rate tables obtained from third-party data providers. Rate tables
for different types of shipments (see below, TL/LTL/parcel) may be
presented in different formats and have different attributes.

Multi-leg or *multistop shipment* is a shipment that has one or more
intermediate stops between the source and destination.

TL/LTL/parcel refers to the type of shipment. *TL (truck load)* refers to a
shipment that completely fills up a truck. *LTL (less-than-truckload)*
refers to a shipment that partially fills up a truck. *Parcel* shipments
are small package shipments that are generally handled through
small package carriers (like UPS/FedEx). The TL rates are generally defined for a lane and for equipment type. The LTL rates are
based on the weight/volume of the shipment in addition to lane and
equipment type, and are defined in $/lb/mile. Most carriers have
published base rates for TL/LTL and negotiate for the discounted
rates based on projected business. As fuel prices vary, prenegotiated
fuel surcharges are added to the carrier invoices. Parcel operators
do not have any standardized rate charts for shipping lanes. Parcel operators use zones, weight of shipment, and service level for
determining the cost of shipment. The zone is decided based on
origin–destination pair and generally is a function of distance between the two. For example, for shipments originating on the East-
ern Seaboard, most of the West Coast destinations will fall in zone 7
or 8 with other destinations in the intermediate zones. For a specific
zone, the parcel rates are published by weight and service level.
Service level refers to the type of service selected for the shipment,
such as two-day delivery, ground delivery, or next-day delivery.

Zone skipping is the process of shipment planning where retailers typically consolidate individual orders into a cheaper TL/LTL load terminating near a parcel carrier's distribution center. The shipment is then split into individual parcels and carried by the parcel carriers for delivery. The parcel rates depend on the zone, which reflects the distance between an origin and destination, and zone skipping provides the shipper with an option to cut costs of the parcel shipments to individual customers.

Multimodal shipment refers to shipments that have mixed modes, such as rail/truck or ocean/rail, to complete the shipment from source to destination. The business process and solution requirements for such shipments differ from single-mode shipments. Multimodal shipments are more complex to plan, rate, and execute. Such shipments have multiple providers managing a single shipment, and that requires enhanced system integration and messaging capabilities across all partners to make sure that the shipment is properly tracked and visible to all parties at all times. Ocean and rail shipments may also need additional third-party services to manage yard operations.

Drayage in the transportation planning context refers to the management of ocean containers at the source, or destination ports, or rail yards. Drayage service providers take ownership of the containers on behalf of the shipper/carrier, and manage them from the port to any specified in-land point as the process moves through docking, unloading, and customs clearance. Similar services cover the rail-yard operations as well.

Customs brokers are service providers that manage the customs clearance of merchandise at the port for imports and exports. These companies create and manage the customs paperwork, settle customs and import duties, and sometimes also coordinate with the drayage companies to clear the containers from the port.

Routing guide is a document published by the shippers as guidelines for their suppliers to select and use carriers for shipments when the shipments are not being managed directly by the shipper. The shipper may audit the suppliers for compliance with the routing guide.

Accessorial charges are additional miscellaneous charges incurred on a freight invoice, and are reimbursable. Examples of such charges are expenses incurred due to delays in loading/unloading, an unscheduled overnight halt at the shipper's facility, a special tarp cover during rain, and so on. These charges are generally part of the carrier contract and are prenegotiated.

Fuel surcharge is the difference applied to the carrier invoice due to the changes in the cost of fuel *after* the carrier's rates were published or negotiated. These can be applied nationally or can be regional.

Mileage/mileage engine is a software application that calculates the mileage between any two points and can generate routes that are navigable by specific equipment such as overdimensioned vehicles (e.g., 53-foot trailers). Such applications are required for the transportation planning processes, and sometimes are embedded within the larger solution. These applications use map databases that need to be updated to reflect the changes in rail/road network.

Rate engine is a software application that can rate a shipment given the route. Rate engines may be embedded within the transportation planning solutions.

Geo-coding is a process of assigning geographic codes to maps and street addresses. One common example is the map-grids that are printed on maps for easy reference. Geo-coding helps determine the route between two points correctly and also provides alternative ways to create and rate a shipment when the precise street address is not known.

Line-haul charges are the basic charges for long-distance moves and are calculated based on the distance moved and the weight of the shipment. These charges are part of the carrier contracts and/or their published rates. When the distance moved is less than 450 miles, it is generally considered a *short-haul* move.

Container optimization refers to the process of optimizing the containers for ocean shipments. This process may be part of purchase planning or transportation planning. The objective of the process is to ensure optimal container utilization for the ocean legs of shipments. A similar process can be adopted for trailer optimization for road shipments and rail-car optimization for rail shipments.

Common carrier refers to carriers that can be bid for shipping by anyone. These carriers typically will not have a long-term contract with the shipper, and services are limited to a specific shipment that is accepted by the carrier.

Dedicated fleet is the fleet that is dedicated to the retailer. It can be owned or leased.

Domestic Shipping

Domestic shipping is generally a simpler process when compared with international shipping. It may sometimes involve multiple legs and multiple modes, though such shipments will be merely a small proportion of the overall domestic shipments. As no national borders are involved, there is no customs process. The payment terms, in-transit damages, and insurance practices are relatively standardized across the domestic shipping industry;

in most cases, there is no inspection of goods prior to the clearance for shipping the merchandise. Therefore, the domestic shipping planning and execution process is simpler, and closely follows the description provided here. Tracking these shipments is also simpler as there is generally a single partner, and rarely a small number of partners, involved in completing the shipment.

If rail is involved in the domestic shipping, rail-car optimization and rail-yard operations may be involved. Rail-yard operations are generally managed by a service provider other than the carrier, and may require additional points-of-process interfaces to track and follow the shipments.

International Shipping

International shipping typically involves more than one transportation mode and multiple legs to complete the transportation from source to destination. In addition to the transportation complexity, international shipping also involves compliance with global trade terms; customs rules for export and import; special financial and payment terms; and additional coordination with service partners like inspection companies, customs brokers, and drayage companies, to completely track and manage the shipments. This makes these shipments more complex, and requires solutions that are functionally richer.

When ocean lanes are involved in the transportation planning, *container optimization* may be part of the purchasing cycle. Container optimization ensures that the shipping container is fully utilized when it is being paid for full. Container optimization can be done prior to purchase planning to adjust the quantities originating at a specific port to fill the container, or it can be done as part of transportation planning, where multiple orders are consolidated at origin to optimize containers for a specified destination port. If the retailer has a consolidation port at the far shore, smaller orders can be consolidated into containers prior to shipping. If no such consolidation facility exists, it may benefit to complete the containerization prior to confirming the orders.

An ocean shipment planning process has unique characteristics that require additional solution capabilities. For example, ocean shipping frequently involves multiple legs in a mixed-mode manner. Exhibit 7.3 shows a typical ocean shipment. The whole shipment may consist of a road trip from the manufacturing plant to the port, drayage operations at the far-shore port, ocean journey, drayage operations at the near-shore port, and finally rail or road transport to the final destination. Optimizing multi-leg, multimodal shipments makes these processes more complex. The additional partners required to manage ocean shipments, such as the drayage companies, inspection companies, and customs brokers, also makes the process more complex to execute.

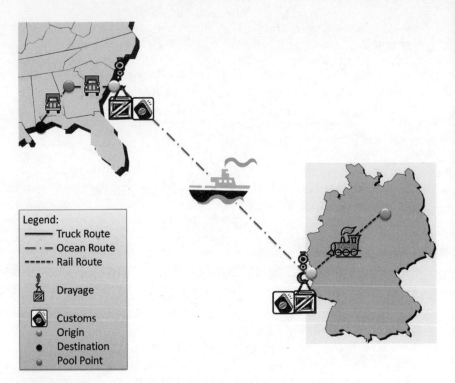

Legend:
— Truck Route
— · — Ocean Route
----- Rail Route
Drayage
Customs
Origin
Destination
Pool Point

EXHIBIT 7.3 Example of an Intermodal Multi-leg Shipment

Inputs and Outputs of the Transportation Planning and Execution Process

Transportation planning and execution processes need the following information as inputs:

- Master data such as items, suppliers, supplier locations, company locations, rates/lanes/routes, carriers, equipment type, carrier contracts, and item/product transportation attributes such as packaging options, weight, volume, department of transportation (DOT) classification, and special handling and transportation requirements
- Orders, which can be purchase orders or material transfer orders
- Tender responses and shipment status messages
- User inputs for configurable options for system processes (such as regions, routes, parameters for consolidation and optimization, and so on).

The process creates the shipments, selects the carriers, tenders the shipments, and tracks them. It provides the following outputs:

- Shipments, load tenders, selected carriers, shipment tracking, rating, and multitudes of electronic messages for interacting with the partners and their systems
- Data, reports, and analytics for tracking the process and measuring process efficiency

Freight Audit and Verification

As shipments are completed and the freight invoices start arriving, the freight audit and verification process kicks in to ensure that these invoices are verified against actual shipments and their statuses, and that the invoices have been computed using the correct shipping rates, fuel surcharge rates, and accessorial charges according to the agreed contract between the shipper and the carrier.

The process also provides the functions for managing any claims against the carrier for loss and/or damage during transit. This is also a good place to execute freight cost allocations, if required. Freight is generally considered to be overhead that is allocated to the underlying cost centers to determine profitability of operations. For example, a retailer may allocate the cost of freight to the stores that are getting the shipments to account for the cost of freight. The cost allocation scenarios will differ among retailers, and depend on their cost accounting methods and the objectives for such allocations.

The freight payment process has two general variations used in the industry. *Match pay* refers to the process of paying for shipments after receiving the invoices from the carrier, and matching them up against authorized/referenced shipments. *Auto pay* is the process where the shipper chooses to pay immediately on completion of a shipment, after obtaining a proof of delivery from the carrier that may come as a final shipment status message.

An overview of the freight payment process is presented in Exhibit 7.4. The freight audit and verification process addresses the following needs:

- Are the carrier invoices raised against the shipments authorized by the shipper?
- Are these shipments successfully delivered and invoices due?
- Did the carrier use the correct rate for the type of shipment, equipment, lane, and weight of the shipment? Are the additional charges aligned with the carrier contracts?
- How are these expenses to be allocated?
- Are there any claims due against this shipment? What are the value and status of such claims?
- Should the invoice be paid in full or in part?

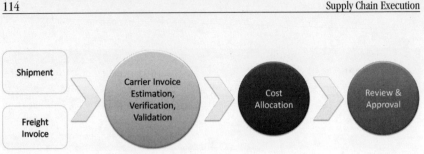

EXHIBIT 7.4 Overview of Freight Invoice Payment

The freight audit process uses the data from the shipments created by the system and the carrier contracts to rate the shipment. When an invoice is received, it is verified against the reference shipment. If the shipment status is configured for payment processing, for example, "delivered" or "closed," then the freight audit process checks all the charges on the invoice and verifies them as valid. For example, the line-haul charges are checked against the shipping rates for the specific lane and shipment type; accessorial charges are validated against the type of charges allowed, and any limits; fuel surcharges are validated against the negotiated rates, and so on. Based on these validations and user configuration, the freight audit process may pass the invoice for payment, reject it, or hold it for user review and approval. Approved invoices are sent to the accounts payable system for action. Based on the payment terms, these can become part of either accrued expenses or payables.

Inputs and Outputs of the Freight Audit and Verification Process

The freight audit and verification process needs the following information as inputs:

- Master data such as vendor locations, company locations, rates/lanes/routes, carriers, equipment type, carrier contracts, and item/product transportation attributes such as packaging options, weight, volume, DOT classification, and special handling and transportation requirements.
- Planned and executed shipments and shipment status messages.
- User inputs for configurable options for system processes and approval workflows.
- In-transit loss or damage information. This is typically received from the receiving applications at the warehouse or stores.

The process creates the list of carrier invoices, which are in approved, held, or rejected status. These can then be integrated with the financial systems as accrued and payable expenses. The process outputs are:

- Status of the freight invoices after verification and audit; approved, rejected, or held for user review.
- Journal entries for the general ledger (GL) or the accounts payable (AP) subledger. Expenses that are accrued but not yet payable are generally represented in the GL journal transactions, whereas those to be processed for immediate payments may be sent to the AP subledger.
- Carrier claims. These will typically involve communicating with the carrier, who can then accept or reject the claim, and final reconciliation of the freight invoice based on the claim disposal. This process is increasingly facilitated using portal environments for ease of collaboration.

Fleet Management

Fleet management is another process within the larger transportation planning and execution business function. Many companies either own their fleet or have a leased fleet dedicated to them. This is common for shipments within their internal network, such as those between their distribution centers and stores. Managing a dedicated fleet requires considerations that may not be relevant to the shipment planning and execution process when the transportation is provided by a common carrier.

Having a dedicated fleet often provides retailers with flexibility in their day-to-day operations for managing store replenishments from the warehouses, as they do not have to go through the tendering process with the carriers.

Following are some of the business functions that go with this process.

Fleet Capacity Planning

This subprocess establishes the required capacity of the dedicated fleet. Using dedicated or own fleet provides scheduling and routing flexibility; if well utilized, it can provide cost savings as well. Managing the fleet, however, can mean additional process overhead to operations.

Fleet capacity planning involves analyzing historical data and projected requirements for shipments between warehouses and stores and other locations within the enterprise supply chain. These requirements may differ by season, and therefore shipment capacity requirements change over time within any given year. The planner may decide to use the average shipment volume numbers, or a base number that guarantees a basic utilization of this dedicated fleet. This target utilization may be anywhere between 60 and 80%. The rest of the capacity fluctuations are then catered to by using the common carriers for internal shipment routes.

Fleet capacity planning addresses the following questions:

- How much capacity should be dedicated?
- Where should this capacity be located?
- What type of equipment should be planned for a dedicated fleet?

The output of the fleet capacity planning exercise establishes the number and type of equipment needed, and the location where this equipment should be housed. As time goes on, the demand may change and dedicated equipment may be moved from one location to another to improve utilization.

Fleet Asset Management

The fleet asset management process provides the asset lifecycle management and asset tracking functionality. Asset lifecycle management consists of planning when an asset is introduced into the system, how the asset is depreciated, when the asset is retired from the system, and the final disposition of the asset.

Asset tracking capability allows managers to locate fleet assets within their facilities, and to ensure optimal asset positioning to support their shipping needs.

Fleet asset management addresses the following questions:

- When/how are assets introduced into the dedicated fleet? How many assets are introduced?
- Where are these assets at any given time (tracking)?
- How should these assets be depreciated?
- What is the retirement schedule for the assets? How will these assets be retired and disposed of?

This function may be part of the fleet management system within the larger transportation process. Alternatively, it can be addressed using the asset management functionality available in most of the ERP applications.

Fleet Maintenance and Scheduling

This process allows for fleet scheduling and regular maintenance. Fleet utilization depends on efficient scheduling. Fleet scheduling is constrained by the availability of drivers and by DOT regulations on the hours of service. Equipment availability at specific locations may further constrain efficient scheduling if these assets are not optimally located.

The fleet maintenance and scheduling function addresses the following questions:

- What is the optimal schedule for a given day for all the equipment in the dedicated fleet? What is the percentage utilization for the dedicated fleet?
- Where is the fleet at a given point in time (real-time tracking)? What type of equipment is available at a given location, and what is its availability?
- Does the process support the capability to create and analyze data required to support regulatory compliance?

Inputs and Outputs of the Fleet Management Process

The fleet management process needs the following information as inputs:

- Master data such as locations, equipment type, item/product, item/product transportation attributes, item/product to location relationships, asset types, asset costs of acquisition and maintenance, asset depreciation parameters, asset active life, drivers, resource availability calendars, and maintenance calendars
- Targeted shipments for the dedicated fleet, and the historical volume of such shipments between facilities
- User inputs for configurable options, such as for compliance and target fleet utilization

The process helps establish the capacity requirements, manage the assets' lifecycles, and schedule and track their utilization. Expected outputs from the process include:

- Fleet capacity requirements by location and by equipment type, and projected utilization
- Asset introduction, maintenance, retirement, and disposal schedules
- Asset operation schedules and utilization reports

Summary

Transportation management processes address the shipping requirements for a supply chain. Transportation planning and execution optimizes the loads, routes, and schedules; helps in determining the best resources and carrier for the lane; provides shipping estimates and validates carrier invoices; and helps in tracking these shipments, thus providing visibility of merchandise in transit. Planning and execution functions can optimize both inbound and outbound shipments.

Freight audit and verification functions validate carrier invoices and establish compliance with the contractual charges and other terms and conditions.

These functions are supported by transportation procurement processes, which were covered in Chapter 5, on supply planning, under the subject of logistics capacity planning.

Fleet management processes support the requirements of managing a private fleet that could be owned or exclusively leased. Managing a fleet requires that these assets are effectively utilized and maintained. Asset management functions support lifecycle management of these assets by planning their introduction, maintenance, and retirement dispositions. Fleet scheduling provides driver management and compliance with government regulations.

CHAPTER 8

Warehouse Management

Warehousing is an equally important component of the distribution equation along with transportation.

Warehouses provide the locations where inventory is stocked primarily to absorb demand fluctuations and to provide smoother operations of the supply chain. Warehouse management processes address the functions required to efficiently manage these operations, such as receiving inventory, stocking and tracking inventory, and shipping it to stores when required.

Most warehouse management solutions create and manage the tasks in the warehouse using the expected inbound and outbound shipments for the day.

The inbound shipments are a result of the purchase orders where the merchandise is inbound to the warehouse from a supplier. These inbound tasks are generally created using the advanced shipping notice (ASN), purchase orders' expected delivery dates, and/or inbound appointments. These inbound shipments create tasks like receiving, staging, cross-docking, and putaway in the warehouse. These inbound shipments or the inbound orders to the warehouse are generally received from the ERP systems, from data-integration gateways, or from other host systems.

The outbound shipments are a result of order fulfillment activities at the warehouse. The stores or other locations raise material transfer or fulfillment requests. These requests are typically generated by the ERP systems or by the replenishment planning applications and processed by an order fulfillment process. The order fulfillment process creates fulfillment orders, or *distribution orders*, which are integrated into the warehouse for execution. The execution of these orders creates picking, packing, and shipping tasks in the warehouse, and the outbound shipments.

Warehouse management helps address the following questions:

- What is the best way to manage all expected inbound (receiving and putaway) and outbound (fulfillment and shipping) operations at a warehouse?

- What is the optimal level of labor in the warehouse? How should the labor be scheduled?
- What is the optimal way to stock the required inventory in the warehouse? How should this be tracked and managed for valuations and loss prevention for own or vendor-owned inventory?

The following industry terms are commonly used in the context of warehouse management:

The *ASN (advanced shipping notice)* is created by the shipper and has information on order reference, shipment details, shipped quantities, and expected date of delivery. It provides an advance notice about the inbound shipments to the receiving party, which helps the receiver to plan and schedule labor and other resources at the receiving location.

The *BOL (bill of lading)* has information similar to the ASN except for the order reference. BOL shows the shipper, consignee, billing party, description of material, transportation class, terms of insurance, and so on. It identifies the contents of a shipment during transit and is also used for triggering carrier claims.

Receiving and *putaway* refer to the inbound warehouse tasks of receiving the merchandise and putting it away for storage.

Pick, pack, and ship refers to the outbound warehouse tasks of picking the orders and packing and shipping the merchandise to fulfill the orders on the warehouse.

Cross-docking is a type of flow within the warehouse where the inbound merchandise is directly sent to the staging/shipping areas for fulfilling an order, and is not stored. Cross-docking has been used by many leading retailers as a supply chain efficiency tool that reduces the inventory in the warehouse, reduces the total lead-time for replenishment to the stores, while simultaneously maintaining order fulfillment rates and service levels. For a detailed discussion on cross-docking, please see the additional coverage of this subject in Appendix C.

Staging is the activity of preparing for the shipment. For example, staging may be done to bring together the entire product that needs to be shipped to a store but must be picked up from several different areas of the warehouse. A *staging area* is normally identified for the purpose of consolidating shipments bound to a single destination.

Slotting is the process of evaluating and determining the best storage location within the warehouse for a given product. The process uses product demand, product handling characteristics, and location attributes to determine the optimal locations.

Interleaving refers to the practice of mixing different tasks in the warehouse such as picking and putaway to obtain maximum productivity. For example, task interleaving can direct a warehouse associate to put away a pallet on her way to the next pick. This reduces travel time, increases productivity, and saves costs due to reduced wear on the equipment and better energy efficiency. Sometimes it is also used with cycle-counting programs to coordinate a cycle count with a picking or putaway task. (Also see the definition of *cycle counting.*)

Consignment inventory refers to inventory that belongs to the supplier, even though it may be stored at a retailer's warehouse. A related term, *vendor-managed inventory (VMI)*, is also used to refer to merchandise that is owned and managed by the vendor even though it may be stocked in a retailer's warehouse. Having vendor-managed inventory in the warehouse helps retailers to reduce their own inventory and hence improve their operating cash flow and inventory turnover. Inventory ownership changes when the retailer decides to ship this merchandise to the store. The warehouse systems typically need integration with the financial systems to pay for the shipped merchandise.

Cycle counting is a type of physical inventory verification. Conventionally, the *physical inventory verification* was planned and executed on a specified day when all the other warehouse activities were suspended. Cycle counting is the process of *continuous* inventory verification without disrupting normal warehouse activities. There are several different processes to plan and execute cycle counting. It may involve conducting cycle counts for a subset of products regularly, or verifying inventory every time a product location is moved and/or inventory for that product becomes too low or zero.

Pick-to-light and *put-to-light* are process enhancements for the picking and putaway processes in a warehouse using lights. As the pickers scan the order/item/LPN, the lights on the correct bin location direct them for picking or for putaway. As the operators do not have to find locations, it increases their productivity and accuracy.

Pick-to-voice and *put-to-voice* are process enhancements for the picking and putaway processes in a warehouse using voice. The pickers are directed by voice for picking or putaway tasks, and need not interact with the RF device using a conventional keyboard or touchpad. As the operators do not have to use a keyboard or touchpad, it provides hands-free operation and increases productivity, accuracy, and safety.

Active locations are warehouse locations that are actively used for order fulfillment. These locations may be closer to the designated staging and shipping areas, with better accessibility and maneuverability. These locations are generally replenished from the reserve locations when empty.

Reserve locations are warehouse locations that are primarily used for bulk storage. These locations are used to replenish the active locations when required.

Order waves refer to batch processing of orders outbound from the warehouse. This process creates the order pick, pack, and ship tasks. (See the order fulfillment subsection under the Outbound Warehouse Operations section in this chapter for more details.)

Engineered labor standards are the performance standards for the warehouse activities. These standards are established using industrial engineering methods and can also be purchased from the data providers. These standards are generally used in warehouse labor planning applications that support labor requirements planning, labor performance management, and performance-based incentive calculations.

Yard management refers to all the functions that help in efficiently using the warehouse yard and docks through better scheduling and visibility. (See the Yard Management section in this chapter for more details.)

MHE (material handling equipment) is the mechanical equipment in the warehouse, such as fork-trucks, -lifts, conveyors, or any other equipment used for loading, unloading, and moving material within the warehouse. Some MHE, such as conveyors, can be interfaced with warehouse management systems and directed dynamically for better warehouse efficiencies.

GS1-128, UCC-128, or *EAN-128* refers to a labeling standard that uses a high-density bar-code. They are all based on the code 128 bar-coding standard that can encode all 128 characters of ASCII and uses double-density coding (encodes two numbers in one character space) for space efficiency on the labels. These codes can be used for pallets or individual packs of products and have information on source, destination, product ID, quantities, order reference, and any other required fields.

RF devices or *handheld/truck-mount devices* are portable mobile devices that are used by warehouse personnel to complete their tasks. These devices connect to warehouse applications using radio-frequency waves. The warehouse management application directs users to their tasks through these devices and also accepts their inputs through a keyboard, touchpad, or scan-guns attached to the device.

Ti-hi refers to the stacking of boxes in a pallet. *Ti* refers to the number of boxes/cases in a layer, and *hi* refers to the number of layers in the pallet. These are sometimes enforced by retailers to keep the standard package sizes that are helpful in better space planning in the warehouse, load planning in transportation management, and inventory handling at the warehouse. Compliance is typically ensured through use of machines at the warehouse inbound receiving operations that measure the weight and volume of inbound shipments.

Dimensioning system refers to machines used in the warehouses that can scan a moving package and produce its dimensions and weight. These attributes are used for optimizing storage and transportation, and to measure supplier compliance with the ti-hi guidelines provided by the retailer.

LPN (license plate number) is an identifier for a container. It contains the container information, including its contents. It is also called a *serialized shipping container label (SSCC-18)*, which is an 18-digit number and bar-code. LPN can be coded at any level, such as container, pallet, or case.

Certified shipping and receiving refers to an agreement whereby the receiving party does not verify the product and quantity received, but rather depends on the scanned information at the time of receiving. This agreement is reached in advance between the shipper and the receiver and makes operations more efficient.

Warehouse management processes can be logically divided into the following process categories.

Inbound Warehouse Operations

These functions address the receiving operations at a warehouse. This is one of the core functions in warehouse management.

Inbound shipments to the warehouse are scheduled so that receiving docks, unloading equipment, and resources can be booked for these shipments. When the shipments arrive at the warehouse, they are unloaded and their disposition is decided. The disposition may involve putaway, staging, or shipping.

Appointment Scheduling and Pre-receiving

The appointment scheduling function allows warehouse operators to schedule inbound shipments in advance. This ensures that the inbound shipments do not have to wait long when they arrive, and that the appropriate dock doors and unloading equipment are reserved for them to be unloaded. Appointment scheduling can also be used for labor scheduling and task planning at the warehouse.

Other *pre-receiving functions* may involve determination of inbound inventory and an optimal disposition for this inventory. In many cases, this inventory is matched against outstanding fulfillment requests, and receiving tasks are paired with the putaway tasks directly to the staging or the shipping areas. This saves storage, putaway, order wave, and order-picking tasks and makes the process more efficient. Though this is highly desirable, its feasibility may depend on the products in the inbound and outbound shipments as well as inventory policies such as first-in-first-out (FIFO) or last-in-first-out (LIFO) and the shelf-life of the products involved.

Receiving and Putaway

These are the actual tasks performed when inbound shipments arrive at the warehouse. Receiving involves unloading the product from the truck and scanning it to record receipt. Scanning also validates the order against which this shipment is being received and helps in reconciling the receipts against the orders. This information is further used to validate invoices for payment to suppliers.

The labels on inbound shipments generally have order information, as well as detailed item information about the shipment. Sometimes the receiver provides the shipping label standards that all suppliers need to comply with. Such labeling standards, if enforced, make the process more efficient as consistent information is encoded on the labels and shipments are easily identified by both the users and the system.

Once unloaded and scanned, the system must determine the disposition of the unloaded products. This disposition determination is generally quite flexible and is based on various system- and user-defined rules. The disposition function creates the putaway task and determines the destination for inbound shipments. When the shipment needs to be put away for storage, the system also suggests a specific location for storing the received merchandise. This selected location is based on the merchandise, existing inventory in the warehouse, empty locations available, material classification of the merchandise, and physical dimensions and stacking attributes of the packaging. The receiver/retailer may also enforce standardized pack sizes for ease of handling and storage. The number of layers in a pallet is also referred to as *standard ti-hi* (tier-height) for pallets/packaging. Ti-hi affects the physical dimensions of the pack, and therefore the storage characteristics.

Some retailers collect such data (size, weight of packs) during the inbound processing of shipments. Such data can be used for planning better transportation and/or to measure compliance with retailers' packaging requirements by the supplier. All inbound shipment packs are sent through a dimensioning system that scans the packs and produces the physical dimensions and weight of the pack.

The destination for putaway tasks may be a shipping dock, staging area, reserve location, or active location.

Inputs and Outputs of the Inbound Warehouse Operations Process

The inbound operations at the warehouse need the following inputs:

- Master data such as warehouse zones, aisles, locations; items, and item attributes like volume, weight, pack sizes, ti-hi, material classification, orientation; vendors, and so on
- Inbound shipments or orders and ASNs
- Labor and equipment data such as resources, availability calendars, skills, performance/efficiency levels, and so on
- Inbound dock doors, number, availability, calendars, and equipment available

The output of the inbound operations processes at the warehouse is:

- The daily schedules for inbound receiving, and putaway tasks, warehouse labor, receiving docks, and equipment required for supporting inbound operations
- Labor requirements and resource schedules
- Inventory receipt transactions as schedules get executed and inbound shipments are received

Outbound Warehouse Operations

These operations at the warehouse result from its role as a fulfillment hub for store or customer orders.

Outbound functions at the warehouse consist of planning all the tasks required to fulfill outbound distribution orders, such as planning for the fulfillment, creating labor schedules to pick merchandise for outbound shipments, packing, route planning, shipping, and so on. These have been logically grouped, and are described below.

Order Planning

This function determines how fulfillment of outbound orders will be executed in the warehouse. Most warehouse management applications run order planning processes that accept a batch of outbound orders and create warehouse tasks to pick and ship the orders. These input orders to the warehouse systems are also called *distribution orders* or *transfer orders*, and are generally integrated into warehouse management systems from an order fulfillment process that collates all outstanding fulfillment requests and determines the best location to fulfill these requests based on warehouse location, request destination, and inventory.

There are two popular methods for order planning in the warehouses:

1. *Batch planning* of orders takes in a group of orders that are ready to be fulfilled. The order lines within this batch are organized according to their location of inventory within the warehouse. Then pick tasks are created so that pickers can move from one aisle to the next and pick all the items required for fulfilling that batch of orders from the current aisle. This allows pickers to be more efficient and not have to go to the same aisle several times to fulfill orders. When multiple order lines are part of a single order, they can be assembled for shipping on the pick-cart or in a separate area subsequently. The number of orders in a batch can be fixed or dynamically change based on the number of items in every order.

2. *Wave planning* of orders also considers a group of orders for fulfillment together. The order lines are divided so that each picker needs to cover only a *part* of the warehouse to finish his or her wave pick tasks. This allows the order waves to be bigger, and the pickers have to travel only to selected aisles of the warehouse. When multiple order lines are part of a single order, the order assembly for wave picks must proceed to the packing station as most likely no single picker will have all the items on an order. Wave planning can be *fixed wave* or *dynamic wave*. The difference is that the fixed waves are completely picked before they are sent to the packing station, while the dynamic waves send the items for packing as soon as a single order is completely picked.

Various considerations affect the selection of batch- or wave-based order planning. Factors that affect such selection are size of the warehouse, number of products in the warehouse, order profile (whether most of the orders are single line or multiple line), as well as demand for the most popular items compared to average demand.

The output of the order planning process is warehouse tasks for picking, packing, and shipping orders.

Task Scheduling and Tracking (Batch/Wave)

As mentioned, the output of the order planning process is the warehouse tasks for picking, packing, and shipping. Depending on the order planning method used, batch or wave, it will create *batch* or *wave picking* tasks. Similar to the order planning definitions above, batch picking involves picking of several orders simultaneously with the objective to reduce the number of picks from a specific location for a specific product. Wave picking divides all the pick tasks so that a specific picker needs to cover only a few zones in the warehouse. Pick tasks allow the order items to be picked and sent to the next station, where pack tasks are executed. In some cases, additional tasks such as gift-wrapping or monogramming are also done at the shipping warehouse. Such tasks are typical of warehouses shipping individual customer orders from a multichannel retail operation. The loading and shipping tasks follow the pick and pack operations to complete the outbound shipment process.

Once the tasks have been created, the warehouse management system continuously tracks them for completion; users can be directed from one task to the next, dynamically, based on current workload and status of the scheduled tasks.

Outbound Load and Shipments Planning

Final shipments from the warehouse can be any one of the following types: parcel, LTL, or TL. Parcel shipments are staged for the parcel carriers to pick up. Others are planned as part of the warehouse management process, loaded, and shipped.

The objective of the shipment planning process is to produce the optimal loads to utilize the trucks effectively, and to route them in the most efficient fashion. In some cases, as for shipments from warehouse to stores, this will require creating multistop loads for smaller loads.

Load and route planning can be done at the warehouse after shipments have been staged, or before pick task planning. Creating loads and routes for outbound shipments can be driven by warehouse applications, where order waves are run, the pick tasks are created, and the shipments are planned using these results. Alternatively, the same objective can be achieved by planning the shipments first, and then running the order waves for the orders in each of these shipments. Whereas reconciliation between planned and executed schedules is required for both alternatives, the latter is more prone to deviations because it does not account for available inventory in the warehouse prior to creating shipments.

Order fulfillment execution frequently spans warehousing, transportation, and order management processes. As a result, it needs all three applications (warehouse management system, transportation management system, and order management) for supporting the whole process. There are several possibilities for integrating the order fulfillment, transportation planning, and warehousing functions. Each of these possibilities has its advantages and challenges. The actual integration deployment decisions vary based on several factors, such as solutions compatibility, ease of integration, solution vendors, and maturity of fulfillment business processes within the organization.

Shipping Labels and Documentation

Shipping documentation management is integral to outbound shipments from the warehouse. There are various types of shipping-related documents that warehouses have to deal with.

The first, of course, is the *shipping* and *packing labels*. Shipping labels serve different purposes for different types of shipments. For a parcel shipment, the shipping label has the address for delivery, name of the recipient, and all parcel service information such as service level, account number to be charged, tracking number, gross weight, shipper, and so on. The packing labels for end customer shipments contain order details and any instructions for the consumer such as directions for returns.

Shipping and packing labels may have specific requirements and these may be specified by the shipper or warehouse operators. For example, a warehouse managed by third-party logistics (3PL) may have several labeling requirements for each of its shipper clients.

For shipments bound for internal locations, or for a business partner, the shipping label may simply have the information about the order being fulfilled by this shipment, and shipment details to help the receiving party scan the label and reconcile with their own order information. These labels may be created at any level, such as cases, boxes, pallets, or truck/container. These cases, boxes, pallets, or truck/container may also be identified by the license plate number (LPN). The shipper and receiver would agree in advance on the contents of the label, and the level of the LPN at which the labels will be printed. Such common practices make it easier for both parties to reconcile the ordering, fulfillment, and receiving processes. Common practices, like labels, can also serve to provide the certified shipping process. *Certified shipping/receiving* can save a lot of time during receiving and validation, as the receiver can simply scan to collect all the information about the shipment, and skip physical validation of quantities and product received.

An *ASN (advanced shipment notice)* is another document created at the time of shipment execution. This document contains information about the order being fulfilled, and details of individual products, shipped quantities, and expected date of delivery. The ASN is addressed to the recipient, and therefore a single shipment may have several ASN documents. The main objective of the ASN is to provide advance notice about the shipment to the receiving party to schedule the receiving resources, as well as trigger any other processes at their end that need a ship confirmation. ASN is very often an electronic document using EDI transaction 856.

The *BOL (bill of lading)* is another shipment-related document that is created in the warehouse for all outbound trucks. The BOL has a lot of information similar to the ASN, but does not require the order reference. The

BOL provides information on shipper, consignee, billing party, description of material, transportation class, terms of insurance, and so on. The BOL serves the purpose of identifying the shipment contents during transit, and is signed by the consignee and the driver when the shipment is received for purposes of *carrier claims*. A shipment can have multiple BOLs.

Invoices for the outbound shipments may be required, especially in third-party logistics (3PL) environments. If so, the warehouse management system needs to have the functionality for billing.

Other shipping documents may be required to cover special situations, such as *hazmat* documentation for merchandise that is classified as such.

Inputs and Outputs of the Outbound Warehouse Operations Process

Outbound operations at the warehouse need the following inputs, some of which are in common with the inbound operations process:

- Master data such as warehouse zones, aisles, locations; items, and item attributes like volume, weight, pack sizes, ti-hi, material classification, orientation; vendors, and so on
- Outbound shipments or orders; user parameters for order fulfillment priorities and the execution process
- Labor and equipment data such as resources, availability calendars, skills, performance/efficiency levels, and so on
- Inventory availability, on hand as well as projected status of inventory based on expected receipts, and purchase orders
- Dedicated fleet assets at the location, and their attributes and availability
- Outbound dock-doors availability, calendars, and available equipment

The outputs of the outbound operations processes at the warehouse are:

- Order fulfillment plan; picking, packing, and shipping tasks; schedules for outbound shipping docks, equipment, fleet, drivers, and so on
- Inventory shipment transactions as the outbound shipments are executed
- Outbound shipments paperwork such as ASN, BOL, labels, and so on

Warehouse Inventory Management

Due to their role in the supply chain, warehouses have significant inventory costs. Inventory management in the warehouse primarily refers to the processes for keeping the inventories accurate. The process of inventory planning, which actually determines the amount of inventory desirable to be maintained at any warehouse, is a separate process that is covered under the Inventory Planning section in Chapter 5.

Maintaining inventory accuracy at warehouses is mostly achieved by using automated systems that reduce errors during receiving, storage, and shipping. Technologies that help in such error reduction are bar-codes, scanning devices, radio frequency ID (RFID) tags, and technologies that use light or voice for directing warehouse operators.

Inventory management processes in the warehouse provide the following:

- They ensure that inventories are accurate.
- They help in inventory valuations, cost allocation (overheads) for warehouse services, and cost transfers for reconciling inventory transfers.
- They provide a means for managing the inventory layers (safety stock, allocated inventory, available inventory, etc.) and the inventory ownership (inventory owned by the retailer versus that owned and managed by the vendor).

Inventory Counts

Inventory counts provide a method for physical verification of all inventories in the warehouse. There are two primary methods for inventory counting:

1. *Physical inventory counting* is the traditional method in which a physical inventory count is scheduled, generally well in advance. On the specified day, all normal warehouse operations are stopped, and all operators are provided with their zone information for physically verifying the inventory in the warehouse against the inventory in the system. Operators move from bin to bin and aisle to aisle, verifying the items and their quantities until the whole warehouse is covered. As warehouse management technologies mature, this method is becoming less popular due to its inherent design, which is disruptive to warehouse operations.

2. *Continuous inventory counting* achieves inventory verification as part of operators' daily scheduled tasks. These tasks are planned and scheduled evenly across time and products to ensure that all inventories in the warehouse are verified at an acceptable frequency during the year. Some of the warehousing systems also allow user-configured rules to continuously generate inventory-counting tasks as part of regular warehouse operations. For example, a rule-based inventory counting task may be generated when a user picks a product and the system determines that the quantity for that product in that location has fallen below a user-set threshold. The system then directs the operator to verify and confirm the quantity in that location. Other rules may trigger

such tasks when the user does not find the correct item in the system-directed location, or puts away a product in a new (empty) location. Such system-based inventory tasks triggered by user-configured rules make inventory counting more efficient and less repetitive, and do not require any disruption in warehouse routine.

Inventory counts result in *inventory adjustments*. These adjustments revise existing inventories downward or upward. They not only change the inventory count, but also affect the financial value tied to the inventory. Depending on the amount of changes and/or cost of inventory adjustment transactions, these changes are either made immediately by the operator or listed for later review and approval by a supervisor.

Inventory Valuation

Inventory valuation is strictly a financial process. However, it helps to understand the process from the warehouse management point of view, as substantial amounts of enterprise inventory are in the warehouse.

The inventory valuation process establishes the value (cost) of inventory at the warehouse. This may be different from the actual cost paid to the supplier for several reasons: It may be averaged across suppliers and time; it may have other cost factors to reflect the handling and storage at the warehouse; or it may have overhead expenses added to it for maintaining the distribution infrastructure. Inventory valuation uses several different methods, some of which are named here with a brief description. It is important to determine the value of inventories for several reasons:

- Inventory valuation is used to determine the cost of transfer when inventories are moved from warehouse to store. As each of these locations are represented as a cost center in the general ledger, all material movements among the locations result in corresponding financial entries.
- It helps corporations understand the profitability of the products.
- It helps in understanding inventory turnover ratio, and its effect on operating cash flow.

Standard costing is the process of establishing the cost of inventory using averages of purchase costs of the product across all suppliers over a set period of time. The standard cost is computed using a predefined amount of historical data in time, and remains unchanged until the next iteration. All inventories are then valued at the established standard cost during the defined period and revised when a new standard cost becomes available.

The *moving average* process is similar to the above process and uses moving averages to compute the standard cost.

Flow policy–based costing varies to reflect the cost of inventory as it was purchased. It is more complex to track and requires enhanced application functionality but also provides true costs. Two commonly used methods are *first-in-first-out (FIFO)*, and *last-in-first-out (LIFO)*. As the name suggests, FIFO uses the oldest inventory to fulfill the orders, and every order is valued at the cost of the inventory that is used to fulfill it. LIFO uses the latest inventory to fulfill and value the orders.

Retail costing is a popular method of inventory valuation in the retail industry. In this method, the inventory is valued at the retail price (i.e., the price at which the retailer sells the product) to reflect the true market value of inventories, rather than the cost of purchase. The problem with this method is that retail price of a product changes frequently with time due to seasonal fluctuations as well as promotions and clearance events. Accounting for these changes in retail prices requires relatively complex computation processes and needs sales histories, price history, price changes, and event data for clearance, promotions, and discounts.

Inventory valuations themselves do not affect the warehouse operations. However, inventory adjustments resulting from inventory counting require that the actual cost of inventories reflects the corresponding financial impact of such adjustments.

Inputs and Outputs of the Warehouse Inventory Management Process

Inventory management at the warehouse needs the following inputs. Most of the master data requirements remain common with the other processes. However, inventory valuation and adjustments require additional data from the enterprise financial systems.

- Master data such as warehouse zones, aisles, locations, items, vendors, and so on
- Costs and costing methods for the merchandise at the warehouse
- Inventory-counting schedules for physical inventory, or rules for creating inventory-counting tasks within regular warehouse tasks
- Approval workflows and rules for inventory adjustments

The outputs of the inventory management process at the warehouse are the following inventory transactions, which are sent to the ERP system:

- Inventory adjustments, quantities, and value by specific products

Yard Management

The yard management functions take care of the activities outside the four walls of the warehouse buildings.

Yard management provides the execution functions for the scheduled appointments, typically at a warehouse. It supports inbound appointments and check-in and checkout processes, manages the dock-door scheduling, and extends inventory visibility to the yard. The appointment scheduling function was covered earlier under the warehouse inbound operations as one of the pre-receiving functions, while the other functions are presented here.

Yard management functions address the following questions:

- Who is currently in the yard waiting for loading or unloading? What orders and inventory are waiting in these trailers? Are there opportunities for last-minute allocation of this inventory that would make warehouse operations more efficient?
- How many live or drop trailer shipments are waiting in the yard, and how can the waiting time and associated charges be desirably managed?
- How can the waiting times for specific trailers be managed before they are worked on? How can it be ensured that the waiting times are within the SLAs with the carriers and vendors?
- How can parking lot space be used optimally to enhance efficiency of warehouse operations?
- What dock doors are available? What type of equipment can be handled at these docks? What resources are required to schedule the dock for unloading or loading activity and what is their availability?

Various smaller functions that together constitute the yard management, and help answer these questions, are as follows.

Gate Management

Gate management is a subfunction of yard management. As trucks arrive or leave the warehouse, they check in or check out at the gate. This process registers incoming and outgoing shipments, and provides visibility to warehouse operators regarding orders that are waiting in the yard for loading or unloading as well as shipments that have left the warehouse.

This also allows warehouse operations to treat the *live loads* and *drop-shipments* differently, optimally using the parking space in the yard and ensuring that trailers that need to be worked on immediately are parked nearest to the docks with unrestricted access for the *yard-jockey*.

Live loads are inbound shipments that need to be unloaded immediately. The tractors for live loads typically wait during the unloading, and the empty trailers are immediately checked out of the warehouse. *Drop-shipments* are shipments where the trailers are dropped off with the tractors leaving to pick up other scheduled loads.

A *yard-jockey* is a person in the warehouse with a tractor to pull trailers from the yard to the loading and unloading docks.

Gate management also helps secure the warehouse by verifying the credentials of all inbound shipments, and ensuring that only authorized shipments are allowed inside, occupying valuable yard area, and that they can be directed to an appropriate area of the yard based on their priority.

Dock-Door Management

Dock-door management targets optimal usage of the warehouse dock doors for inbound as well as outbound operations. Dock doors can become a real constraint in the warehouse, and this function provides for scheduling them in advance of actual loading and unloading activities, along with the right equipment and labor available, when a trailer is being worked on. The primary objective of dock-door management is to ensure that the dock doors are utilized as planned, that they do not become a constraint and hamper the warehouse's ability to execute, and that they always provide visibility for the currently available dock capacity as unplanned changes to the schedule happen in real time.

Yard Inventory Visibility

Yard inventory visibility tells the warehouse operators what orders are waiting in the yard, where these trailers are located, and what merchandise is contained in these trailers. This visibility into the yard allows operators to react to urgent material requests or opportunistic cross-docking functions when the contents of a trailer can be directly sent to staging and shipping areas.

The inventory picture in the yard is created from the checked-in trailer information and the shipments on these trailers. These shipments are matched to the ASNs in the system and detailed inventory information is thereby made available.

Inventory visibility for the trailers in the yard can also feed enterprise supply chain visibility, providing flexibility to inventory planners and merchants for last-minute adjustments to their purchasing, distribution, and allocation plans.

Inputs and Outputs of the Yard Management Process

Yard management at the warehouse needs the following inputs:

- Master data for dock doors, equipment, capacity, calendars, yard locations and their attributes, for a given warehouse.
- Rules for appointments, checking in, and checking out; approval workflows, if required.

■ Inbound orders/ASNs. While yard management in isolation may not need this information, it enhances the visibility of inventory in the yard.

The outputs of the yard management process produce the check-in plan, checkout plan, dock-door and equipment schedules, yard utilization plan, and inventory visibility.

Warehouse Labor Management

The complexity and cost of labor can vary based on the size and activities performed at the warehouse. However, labor constitutes the largest variable expense at any warehouse, and labor planning, scheduling, and tracking has become a well-established process that is also supported by most of the leading warehouse management systems. In fact, simply optimizing the labor usage in a warehouse can sometimes provide enough return on investment (ROI) to justify automation of a facility using systems and technology.

The warehouse labor management process addresses the following:

■ What is the labor requirement for planned inbound and outbound operations for current and near-projected periods?
■ Are available resources sufficient? Should additional resources be scheduled? Should additional workshifts be scheduled?
■ What is the total workload on any given day? How is the schedule progressing in real time? How much work is completed and how much is remaining? What is the resource utilization, and individual efficiencies? What is the estimated time when all scheduled activities can be completed?
■ What is the resource–skill matrix available and required? Which are the best-skilled resources? Which resources need training?

Labor management consists of the following main capabilities.

Engineered Labor Standards

Engineered labor standards are based on industrial engineering studies that establish the standard expected time to finish a number of common activities in a warehouse. For the purpose, these activities are decomposed into smaller components that can be standardized based on parameters such as equipment used, type of pallet, type of move, skill of the operator, and so on.

These standards are used to schedule labor in the warehouse for the projected type and number of tasks on any given day. This allows the warehouse manager to make sure there is enough labor available for planned tasks. The available labor may come from permanent warehouse employees and/or contract workers, and by extending shift hours.

Engineered labor standards can also be used for calculating worker efficiency, and incentive pay if desired.

Labor Reporting and Tracking

Real-time task tracking is an important aspect of the labor function in the warehouse. It allows managers to see the total amount of work planned, completed, and remaining for the day. With proper equipment and systems, it can track all the activity in the warehouse on a real-time basis, allowing the supervisor to manipulate resources, hours, and equipment to ensure that planned warehouse tasks are on track for completion by the end of the day.

Labor reporting provides inputs on skills and efficiency of the operators. This can be used for incentive calculations, training, and labor planning and simulation.

Inputs and Outputs of the Warehouse Labor Management Process

Labor management at the warehouse needs the following inputs:

- Shared master data as mentioned earlier for the other warehouse processes
- Inbound shipments or orders, and ASNs
- Outbound (transfer) orders
- Labor and equipment data such as resources, availability calendars, skills, performance/efficiency levels, and so on.
- Engineering standards data for warehouse activities and their components

The outputs of the labor management processes at the warehouse are:

- The labor schedule for daily operations
- Projected labor requirements for the immediate future based on the expected warehouse load
- Progress reporting on warehouse activities
- Resource utilization, efficiency, rates, and incentive information

Slotting Optimization

Slotting optimization is the process of determining the best storage locations for the merchandise carried in the warehouse. Locations in the warehouse can be assigned using multiple criteria. Locations can be static, where a specific product is always in the same location, or they can be dynamically determined based on the current warehouse configuration and location availability.

Some obvious parameters for determining the storage location in a warehouse are product dimensions, weight, orientation, and handling attributes, and the product class (e.g., hazmat may not be stored in the same place as other products).

Then there are parameters that are less obvious but equally important in determining the product locations in the warehouse. Examples of these factors are demand, distance from dock doors, and handling requirements. Moreover, these factors can change over time and require frequent evaluation. The product demand can change due to seasonality and trends. In response to the changes in demand, the number and types of warehouse operations (receiving, picking, etc.) also change. However, there are only a fixed number of locations in the warehouse with the most desirable attributes such as being close to the docks, easily reachable, eye-level storage, and so on. The objective of slotting is to optimally select these most desirable locations for products that will have the highest number of operations so that operator and process efficiency can be maximized.

The slotting optimization process evaluates the current warehouse locations, historical and projected demand patterns, product attributes, and user constraints to come up with optimal locations for storage within the warehouse. When slotting is integrated with the warehouse labor applications, it can also create a list of additional activities or moves required in the warehouse to get to this optimal configuration, and the associated labor cost for executing these moves. The user can then review the recommendations and decide whether to follow or ignore the suggestions.

Batch slotting optimization processes run independently of the warehouse management systems, at fixed intervals, to create the recommended changes and the additional slotting-related tasks. This requires integration with the warehouse management system for historical receipts and shipments; current warehouse layout and locations; and current on-hand inventory information to determine the viability of locations. It may also use the projected receipts and shipments if available. As above, the recommendation is generally reviewed by a user and may be adopted fully or in part.

Continuous moves slotting optimization is an enhanced slotting process that can dynamically change storage locations as demand patterns change. Continuous slotting algorithms dynamically recommend new locations as merchandise is received and shipped to change the storage configuration of the products in the warehouse. As minimal moves are specifically required to make such changes, it can be a more productive way of achieving the slotting optimization.

Inputs and Outputs of the Warehouse Slotting Process

Slotting optimization at the warehouse needs the following inputs:

- Shared master data as mentioned above for the other warehouse processes
- Inbound and outbound shipments or order history, and the projected volume for these transactions
- Warehouse activity/task rates to compute the costs of slotting moves, and resources required

The outputs of the labor management processes at the warehouse are:

- The optimized configuration for stocking
- Slotting moves, with cost and resource projections

Billing Management and Cost Allocation

Billing management as a function of warehouse management is limited to facilities run by 3PL (third-party logistics) companies.

The cost allocation function for warehouse activities is common to all retailers. Cost allocation is used to add the handling and storage costs to the basic cost of the merchandise flowing through the warehouse to reflect warehouse maintenance expenses.

These two functions are presented together because the underlying concepts for both are very similar. Both the processes can leverage an activity-based costing model for the warehouse that reflects the handling costs as a shipment passes through the warehouse.

In an enterprise context, billing management has no direct relevance, but the cost allocations process provides corporations with an objective basis to allocate the warehousing overheads to other functions that use these services. This creates a better COGS picture, as well as allowing the enterprise to analyze the costs of operations with objective data rather than using rough estimates for the warehouse cost structures. For retailers, the costs of distribution can add up to 10 to 15% of their total costs, and understanding the warehousing costs provides them with better profitability analysis and opportunities for cost savings.

Billing Management

The billing management function provides 3PL service providers with the ability to invoice their customers for warehouse services provided.

The process consists of identifying all the warehouse transactions and associated costs to these transaction types to determine the cost of the warehouse activity for a customer. Examples of such transactions are receiving, putaway, picking, packing, loading, cycle counting, shipping, and so on. As a shipment passes through the warehouse, these warehouse transactions are captured and persisted for every activity related to the stocked merchandise. Storage costs are added to these activity-based costs using the storage location and the number of days the merchandise is stored in the warehouse. In a warehouse run by 3PL, contracts with various clients may have several definitions of the warehouse activities and their related costs, along with different service-level agreements. To handle such varying calculations, rules and formulas can be defined into the system, supporting this function to automatically create correct invoices for different clients using their contract rates and negotiated discounts.

The rules and formulas make it possible for the 3PL company to use a single system for managing the warehouse and still provide different service levels to different clients based on their SLAs, contractual agreements, and volumes.

Cost Allocation

The cost allocation function helps companies to establish the true cost basis for distribution expenses toward calculating their total cost of goods sold (COGS). Almost all companies use some method of allocating warehouse costs among the product categories, departments, and any other organizational user groups so that the cost of operations is supported by all who need the warehousing services. This helps companies to accurately measure the contribution (profitability) of their products and evaluate their portfolios.

These allocation methods are conventionally based on the value of the merchandise in the shipment, and specified as a percentage of this value. However, the handling costs often depend on the handling characteristics of the merchandise rather than the value. For example, a shipment of outdoor furniture that requires manual handling using a forklift will almost always consume more distribution resources compared to another shipment of similar value (like electronics) that is conveyable on a mechanized belt.

To accommodate the handling characteristics, sometimes the distribution charges can be estimated and allocated using the weight or volume as the basis for such allocation. In this scenario, a certain percentage of the value of the shipment will be allocated as handling charges based on the weight or volume of individual lines in that shipment. Other handling characteristics like material convey-ability (requires a fork-lift operator or conveys on a belt) are difficult to model, though these can provide more realistic basis for the allocation of warehouse handling costs.

To model such handling characteristics, the merchants can sometimes create material handling categories for items. Depending on the category to which an item belongs, a certain predefined percentage of its value is considered as distribution cost, and allocated accordingly. This allows modeling categories like furniture, which requires more handling resources, to bear a higher share of handling costs, compared to merchandise like electronics, which may be of similar value but do not consume similar handling resources. Offsetting these costs through category-based rules may work to some extent but still remains a subjective process.

There remains a huge gap between the allocated cost and the real cost of warehouse operations on a specific shipment as it passes through the warehouse. The gap arises due to various factors, such as their handling characteristics, stocking requirements, cross-docking opportunities, and relative storage locations within the warehouse.

An activity-based costing model for warehouse cost allocations solves most of the above issues. It is a superior process, and it allows for a more accurate cost basis for warehousing services. Such a costing model will require two basic inputs:

1. The first part of the activity-based costing requires that all the warehouse tasks are coded and rated. As part of the regular warehouse management, most warehousing applications track all the activities at a very granular level. These activities have data not only on the task, but also on the associated order that is being received or shipped. The order data associated with the warehouse task then permits associating the actual task and its cost to the merchandise being worked on. Based on how many times merchandise is touched before it is shipped out, the warehousing costs will vary.

2. The second part of warehouse costs is the storage costs. These costs depend on the number of days for which a product is stored in the warehouse and the amount of space it takes up. The number of days during which a product stays in the warehouse is easy to calculate when the products have a batch number or some other way to track the individually received shipments, such as tracking the original LPN or case ID. A FIFO/LIFO-based inventory allocation method may help as well. In absence of any batch tracking, there is a possibility of using an average number of storage days for product categories that is calculated using historical data. The second part of storage cost information, the volume and type of storage, is easier to determine as these are available as standard product attributes at the warehouse.

Inputs and Outputs of the Billing Management and Costing Processes

The inputs are:

- Shared master data as mentioned above for other processes
- Warehouse activity/task codes and rates
- Daily warehouse transaction data for all activities
- Inventory costing data (if required) for any allocation algorithms/rules

The outputs of the billing/cost management processes at the warehouse are:

- Invoices for billing management (specifically applicable to warehouses run by a 3PL company)
- Cost allocations for the warehousing operations among the organizational units that benefit from these operations, such as stores

Summary

Warehousing aspects of a supply chain are addressed by the warehouse management processes. Inbound operations at a warehouse include the appointments, disposition planning, receiving, and putaway processes. Outbound operations at a warehouse include order fulfillment planning, fulfillment task scheduling and tracking, and outbound shipments planning and execution.

As warehouses stock the inventory in transit from the vendors or manufacturing plants to stores and customers, inventory management processes for maintaining an inventory ledger, inventory valuation, and inventory counting are also supported by the warehousing functions.

Labor management in the warehouse requires ability to plan, schedule and track labor. Sometimes these functions may be extended to support time, payroll, and incentive management for warehouse labor.

Slotting processes in a warehouse enable it to evaluate existing allocated locations with respect to the warehouse activities of receiving and shipping, and provide alternative assignments in an effort to reduce warehouse labor requirements to sustain expected service levels.

The warehouse management processes help an organization to effectively manage inventories and provide targeted service levels for replenishment of downstream locations in the supply chain.

CHAPTER 9

Reverse Logistics Management

Reverse logistics management covers all the business functions that allow a retailer to process the merchandise returns generated at the stores, web sites, or warehouses. Reverse flow of merchandise can begin as:

- Retail customer returns at a store, and online or catalog returns at a returns facility.
- Vendor buybacks, which can be a result of new product introduction by a vendor in a category, or a competitive replacement of another vendor's product. Such buybacks may be triggered by merchants after appropriate negotiations with their suppliers. The buyback information is sent to the stores as part of daily action items to facilitate scheduling and execution of the related tasks.
- Retailer-initiated returns due to quality, safety, or compliance concerns. These returns can be triggered by merchants based on customer complaints, vendor request for callback, or a regulatory agency issuing a product callback.

Regardless of their starting point, the returns need to be managed so that the associated costs are minimized. Examples of such costs are the cost of handling returns at the store or for a web/mail channel, determining disposition, transportation, disposal-on-site, and financial reconciliation of the returns transactions.

The first step for customer returns may happen in a store in case of physical returns, or at a call center where online and catalog customers call for getting a return merchandise authorization (RMA). This chapter focuses only on the supply chain aspects of returns management, and ignores the customer interaction part of the process.

Reverse logistics management consists of managing the flow of merchandise from stores and customers back to the supplier. This returned merchandise may pass through a consolidation center. The complete returns transaction can contain a few shipment legs, warehousing, packing,

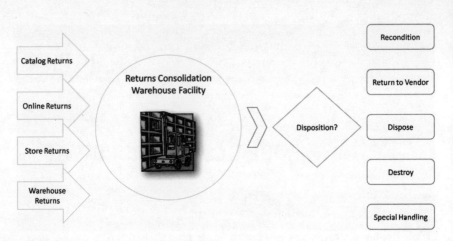

EXHIBIT 9.1 Overview of Reverse Supply Chain Process

handling, and other warehouse activities. Due to the complexity of managing the reverse flow, many companies simply subcontract the reverse logistics to a third-party logistics provider. These contracts may be limited to transportation and warehousing, or may include all services, such as disposition determination, disposal, and supplier credit reconciliation.

An overview of the process is presented in Exhibit 9.1.

Returns Disposition Determination

The returns disposition process helps determine the best way to dispose of the returned merchandise. The disposition can take many forms:

- The returned merchandise can be returned to the sales floor. It may need testing, reconditioning, repackaging, and restocking. It may or may not be marked down for clearance. This disposition action can result in store activities or shipping to a reconditioning facility, and tracking the merchandise back through to the sales floor. The markdown pricing decision may be derived from a corporate policy, or simply may be a store manager's privilege.
- It can generate a return to vendor (RTV) transaction. Such a disposition can then generate many supply chain activities, such as shipping back to a returns consolidation center or directly to the vendor. The process will also mean integration with accounting to adjust supplier accounts based on the terms of the returned merchandise.
- It can result in a decision to dispose of the returned merchandise. The disposal can be onsite or offsite. Onsite disposal may simply trash the

merchandise in accordance with local regulations. Offsite disposal may be done by a third-party company that clears the disposed-of items on a regular basis from the stores.

- It can result in a decision to destroy the merchandise, onsite or offsite. This is generally a result of regulations in place for certain classes of merchandise.
- It can result in disposal with special handling instructions, such as for merchandise that is considered hazardous. Such merchandise needs to be tracked until it is safely disposed of, and records maintained for state and federal regulatory agencies.

Inputs and Outputs of the Returns Disposition Process

The main inputs to this process are:

- *Merchandise classification and regulations for disposal.* For example, all merchandise that is classified as hazmat or biohazard has special regulations governing its handling, storage, and disposal on return. Other merchandise may have disposition regulations as well. It is important that all disposition decisions comply with these regulations and sufficient records are maintained for verification by the regulatory agencies.
- *Supplier contracts and terms of merchandise returns.* These terms govern whether the merchandise can be returned to a vendor. Sometimes, the logistics costs of returns may be higher than simply disposing of merchandise locally and reconciling the accounts. If the merchandise is returned to the vendor, these terms will determine who bears the cost of transportation, insurance, warehousing, and handling. Suppliers may also agree to provide cost rebates, if the number of such returns is unacceptably high or crosses a prenegotiated level.

The output of the process is the disposition method for the retuned merchandise.

Logistics Planning and Execution for Returns

The supply chain for returns flows in reverse to the main flow of goods. While most companies manage their main supply chain logistics with great care, the reverse flows do not get as much attention.

The destination of merchandise in the reverse supply chain depends on the disposition. Based on the disposition, this merchandise may need to be returned to suppliers for credit/rebates, reconditioned and sent back to the stores, or disposed of.

The reverse supply chains can use a *returns consolidation center*, which is a warehouse specifically for managing reverse flows. The returns consolidation center receives all returns from warehouses and stores. It determines the disposition of the merchandise and plans for the tasks required to complete the execution of the selected disposition method. Physically, this might or might not be a separate facility from the main warehouses.

The majority of customer and store returns to the facility can be parcel or LTL. The store returns can take advantage of the backhaul trucks going to the warehouse. Returns from other warehouses to the returns facility can be optimally planned using the logistics planning systems in most cases.

Once the merchandise reaches the returns consolidation facility, it will be tracked until its final disposal. The next part of the returns logistics chain will take some of the merchandise to the supplier's warehouse. Such returns from the retailer's returns consolidation facility to the supplier's warehouse can also be optimized using the transportation planning systems.

The inputs to the logistics planning and execution process for reverse logistics are the same as for the main supply chain processes. These have been covered in previous chapters.

Financial Reconciliation of Returns

Returned merchandise not only creates a reverse flow of goods, but may also generate a reverse flow of financial transactions. This starts with the credit for customer returns at the store or call center, and continues through the credit and/or rebates from the suppliers to the retailer to compensate for the returned merchandise. Based on the contract terms with the suppliers, returned merchandise can be reconciled in several ways:

- It may simply be written off as loss.
- The transaction may result in a credit note from the supplier to the retailer. The value of the credit note depends on the contractual terms.
- It may result in a rebate or discounts on future purchases from the supplier.

Finally, the credits and rebates may need to be reconciled to calculate the new cost of goods sold (COGS). The financial reconciliation process for returns needs to address all the above situations.

Many companies may insist on uniform treatment of returns with all their suppliers to simplify the financial aspects of returns.

Inputs and Outputs of the Returns Financial Reconciliation Process

The primary inputs to the financial reconciliation for returns are the supplier contracts, return transactions, and their values.

The outputs of the process are the journal transactions registering write-offs, or debit and credit notes to accurately reflect the cost of returned merchandise in the financial journals.

Summary

Reverse logistics management is a smaller but equally important aspect of today's supply chains. It allows the enterprise to manage the returns of merchandise and materials to the vendors that may originate with customer returns, buybacks, quality issues, or other reasons. These processes establish the organizational procedures for determining eligibility and disposition for the returned materials. They also support the reverse logistics for moving these materials and merchandise to the vendor and the financial reconciliation to account for the returns.

PART IV

Supply Chain Collaboration

CHAPTER 10

Collaborative Processes

The heart of supply chain management is the flow of merchandise. Though it is true for most industries, it is more so for retailers as replenishment and distribution are core supply chain competencies in a retail environment.

As replenishment heavily depends on the suppliers and distribution on carriers, well-thought-out partner collaboration can greatly enhance smooth operations for retailers and increase their supply chain efficiencies.

There are many opportunities for supply chain collaboration with partners. These processes (where such collaboration is possible and may be desirable) span from planning through execution and virtually cover the whole supply chain functional scope. The returns and benefits of each of these processes are different, and should be evaluated in specific organizational context.

While CPFR® (Collaborative Planning Forecasting and Replenishment[1]) is the most commonly known collaborative process, the discussion of supply chain collaboration here is not limited to these processes alone. We define *supply chain collaboration* as any process that spans across corporations and therefore provides an opportunity to work collaboratively with the intention of providing better planning, execution, or sharing of information.

Since some of the collaborative processes involve projected future demand and replenishment quantities, the concepts of *planning and execution fences* and *quantity flexes* that relate to such collaboration are helpful to support the understanding of these processes. Planning and execution fences define specific points in time along the collaborative time-horizon. Quantity flexes define the range of percentage change that can happen to the projections.

For example, if the collaborative time-horizon for which the plans are shared with the suppliers is four months, then the parties may agree to

---

[1]CPFR is the registered trademark of VICS (Voluntary Interindustry Commerce Standards).

the first two weeks being a frozen horizon during which the shared demand/supply numbers will not be changed. This is done to ensure that the shared plans are not too volatile and can be effectively used to drive the planning and fulfillment processes at the retailer as well as at the supplier's end. In this case, the frozen planning fence will be two weeks and quantity flex is zero.

The number and length of fences is completely open to be defined between collaborating parties. For example, a retailer may define three fences, where the first fence starts at the current time and lasts through to the first two weeks, with zero or minimal flex; the second fence starts at the end of second week and lasts through next six weeks after the first fence, with flex up to 20%; followed by the final fence, which goes till the end of collaborative period and normally has no flex guarantee. These definitions depend on the type of industry, type of merchandise, demand forecasting accuracy, and quality of relationship between collaborating parties, among other things.

Collaborative Planning Processes

Collaborative planning processes include demand and supply planning. This is one of the collaborative processes where CPFR has created standard industry practices for retail, and some of the more popular industry scenarios. The extent of collaborative planning depends on the partners' trust in each other, confidentiality agreements, volume of business, business relationship history, and objectives driving the collaborative effort. Planning collaboration provides the following opportunities:

- A *joint business plan* can be shared that identifies opportunities for collaboration. Such plans may identify planned store openings and closings, assortment changes, promotions, new product introduction plans, and so on. This can also establish the basic parameters for collaboration, such as horizon, planning fences, flex quantities, and inventory policies or changes to them.
- *Sales forecasts* are sometimes shared with the suppliers if confidentiality is maintained. Sales forecasts help suppliers to plan their own strategic and account management activities.
- *Replenishment plans* can be shared with the suppliers, thus providing them with visibility into the retailer's future projected demand. These plans reflect to some degree the retailer's intent to buy. While the purchase orders still define the actual contract for buying merchandise, these plans provide the future outlook to the suppliers, making it possible for them to adjust their own manufacturing processes to better meet the retailer's demand. A successful deployment of the

replenishment collaboration process between partners can distinctly enhance fulfillment rates, while simultaneously reducing the overall inventory in the system.

Collaborative Execution Processes

Supply chain execution processes offer many more opportunities for collaboration. Unlike the planning processes, where the primary objective of the collaboration is to enhance reliability of the demand and supply plans, the objective of collaboration during the execution phase is to stabilize operations through proactive exception management, resulting in overall efficiency gains for the partners.

This type of collaboration during the execution phase may take the form of automated electronic transactions, state management and definition of specific events when these transactions reach a specified status, identification of process exceptions that need user intervention, proactive alerts generated when these events and exceptions occur, and finally, an automated or manual resolution of the identified exceptions. In addition to the automated transaction-level integration, execution collaboration may utilize conventional portal-based sharing of information to achieve certain functions.

As the execution processes affect the immediate operations, these capabilities provide immediate benefits by automating the transactions and by enabling process management through exceptions.

The following discussion will provide insight into the supply chain execution processes that have the greatest potential for efficient execution through a collaborative approach. Currently available packaged solutions do not necessarily address all these processes, but a well-designed platform-based solution for partner collaboration can be configured to support a large number of situations.

Ordering management through a collaborative process can provide a common venue for the retailer and the suppliers to look for all order-related information and statuses. It also provides an opportunity to define common definitions of status, events, exceptions, and resolutions. The scope of collaboration for ordering generally is limited to the merchandise suppliers and covers the process of purchase order lifecycle management from the creation of purchase orders through their settlement. Purchase orders go through several statuses throughout their lifecycle, and a collaborative process managed through a common portal can provide a single source of information for all the participants. It allows the suppliers to proactively communicate changes to the planned fulfillment to the retailers, mark ready-to-ship orders, and ask for routing instructions, and for retailers to plan for the impact of any last-minute changes to fulfillment plans, publish such changes to other internal systems (e.g., replenishment planning), provide routing instructions to carriers, publish settlement status for carriers and merchandise vendors, and manage invoicing disputes.

Order fulfillment functions cover the actual logistics functions as the merchandise flows through the supply chain. This information is typically obtained from the carriers and other third-party logistics (3PL) partners who manage the transportation and warehousing of the merchandise for the retailer. These functions provide opportunities to track real-time status of shipments, ASNs, warehouse check-in/checkout status, warehouse/yard inventory, receipts at the warehouse, and status of the received inventory at the warehouses or stores.

Carrier management offers yet another set of functions that can be managed in a collaborative environment. Several carrier interactions, such as *carrier bids, load tenders, tender responses, scheduling, shipment status messages, proof of delivery, freight invoices,* and *freight settlement and disputes and claims*, can be efficiently accomplished with automated electronic transactions and an online carrier portal for such collaboration.

Auctions offer another area of collaborative commerce, especially when buyers routinely make use of forward and/or reverse auctions for purchases. In the conventional (or forward) auction process, buyers compete to place bids to obtain merchandise. In reverse auctions, the buyer publishes the purchase requirements and invites the sellers to place bids responding to the buyer's requests. Both types of auctions are prevalent in *business-to-business (B2B)* trading scenarios. Reverse auctions may be open to all, or by invitation, or only to those providers that meet a predefined criterion set by the buyer.

VMI (vendor-managed inventory) is another area where collaboration with the vendors can provide operational efficiencies to the retailers. Vendor-managed inventory consists of the buyer providing demand information to the supplier, and the supplier maintaining agreed inventory levels of the product. The inventory may be maintained either at a store or a warehouse. The inventory location is typically owned and operated by the retailer, while the specific inventory ownership is retained by the vendor. The vendor gets paid for this inventory either when the inventory is sold at the store or when the inventory is shipped from the warehouse to the store. To efficiently operate this model, the exchange of real-time inventory, sales, and shipments (inbound as well as outbound) is very important. A collaborative platform can be used for exchanging this information. This inventory is sometimes called *consignment inventory.*

Offshore inspections are typically conducted by third-party companies to confirm that the goods are ready to be shipped and meet the expected quality of the importer. A collaborative portal-based environment provides an ideal tool for such communication where the importer can update all the orders ready to be inspected and the offshore companies provide the confirmation electronically, which is then relayed to the supplier, clearing the goods for shipping.

Customs clearance and drayage services for imported merchandise are often handled by brokers and drayage companies on behalf of the importers. Ideally, the communication required between the three parties to manage the customs and clear the shipments from the port should be managed through a portal or electronic transaction communication so that all the involved parties are up to date and work together from the same set of documents.

3PL-run warehousing facilities provide another potentially valuable opportunity for a collaborative application between the service provider and the retailer. It ensures that the retailer has real-time information of all inventories in the warehouse, all inbound orders, and all planned shipments.

Vendor returns consist of damaged merchandise, buyback merchandise, or merchandise that has been returned by customers. The process of vendor returns can take many different routes. Some retailers have a consolidation facility where all vendor returns from the stores are consolidated before being shipped back to the vendor. Others may simply notify the vendors of the returns, and the actual responsibility of picking up the merchandise from the warehouse or stores may lie with the supplier. Some retailers subcontract the entire process to a 3PL service provider. In all its variations, this is another process that lends itself to enhanced efficiency through a collaborative approach and supporting technologies.

Collaborative Performance Management

Many corporations evaluate suppliers and carriers on several different metrics targeted to drive process compliance and efficiencies. Suppliers can be measured on fulfillment rates, quality, lead-times, costs, and invoicing accuracy to drive efficiencies, and on EDI failure rates and missed transactions to drive process compliance and automation. Carriers can be measured for compliance on maintaining the scheduled loading and unloading windows, shipment tracking messages, freight invoice accuracy, and timeliness of other EDI transactions.

The metrics measured above can be used for evaluating contracts, renewals or cancelation of new business, and in some cases, chargebacks for costs resulting from the vendor's inability to provide the agreed SLA on operations or process.

Partner scorecarding collaboration provides an opportunity to the enterprise to share this information with its partners. It ensures that the suppliers and carriers are aware of missed service-level targets and can proactively address such situations. When chargebacks are a result of such performance measurement, the platform provides a quick traceback to individual transactions that are the basis of such chargebacks on a self-service basis. It saves the retailers from having to maintain a dedicated dispute-resolution line as most of the chargebacks can be resolved on the portal.

Summary

Supply chains have several opportunities where active collaboration with partners can provide additional benefits, such as reduced cost, increased responsiveness to changes, and visibility across the whole process with no organizational boundary constraints.

Supply chain collaboration processes help in identifying, establishing, and managing such opportunities. Examples where such collaboration adds value can be found in supply chain planning as well as execution processes. Business plans, forecasted sales, and replenishment plans can be selectively shared with partners to enhance supply chain response to changes and to provide visibility. Order management and transportation management are some examples from the execution processes where active collaboration can reduce costs and provide visibility of ordered and in-transit inventory.

Supply Chain Technology

As with all other aspects of an enterprise, technology plays a big role in managing the supply chains. Most technology enables process automation, standardization, and simplification, therefore enhancing process efficiency, organizational productivity, and effectiveness. Technology for supply chains is no different. However, it not only provides automation and process efficiency, but also provides solutions that are qualitatively better, thus extending the benefits to active cost reductions through better planning, execution, and tracking.

This is also a subject too large to be adequately addressed in a chapter of a book that is primarily devoted to describing the supply chain functions rather than the underlying technology. However, the discussion is designed to provide the reader with a general understanding of the technology issues and how these can affect the successful adoption of the supply chain technology and processes.

ERP and Supply Chain Management

The first question to address is, What exactly is the difference between the enterprise resource planning (ERP) systems and supply chain management applications? Many corporations struggle with this issue and it is merely confounded by the fact that these two streams of business applications are quickly merging into one.

ERP systems are simply the forerunners of the supply chain systems. ERP systems started with a smaller footprint, addressing the automation of financial systems, but they have greatly expanded into all business functions. The larger ERP systems today address almost the entire spectrum of business functions required to run an enterprise, including most of the key supply chain functions. However, supply chain solutions have been emerging and are the latest additions to most of the ERP solutions. Therefore, supply chain solutions that are currently offered as part of the larger ERP solutions may not be as mature as some solutions offered by specialized supply chain solution vendors.

That brings us to the discussion of best-of-breed solution providers versus ERP vendors.

Best-of-Breed versus ERP

This is the other technology question that needs to be addressed when enterprises think of investing in supply chain applications. Larger ERP solutions currently support a large number of supply chain functions, and that leads to the logical question, Why should a company look at best-of-breed supply chain solution providers? There is no single right answer, but an objective assessment of needs and expectations should lead most companies in a direction that works for them.

The most compelling argument in support of using the ERP systems for supply chain functions is the common master data and functional integration that may be expected from a single solution from a single provider. In contrast, combining one vendor's ERP with the best-of-breed supply chain solutions from other vendors will almost always require multiple copies of master and transaction data. These multiple copies of the same data must be integrated with each other and kept consistent to ensure the continuous, unbroken system support for various business processes, as these processes will invariably require all of these systems working seamlessly together.

However, supply chain solutions can provide a real differentiator for many companies, and can substantially affect the cost of operations. Therefore, selecting a supply chain solution should be a serious exercise in exploring the corporate goals, evaluating the current processes, exploring the possibilities for improvement, and then selecting a solution that is extensive and flexible enough to allow for these changes. While selecting a best-of-breed solution may present additional deployment challenges through multiple master data repositories and application integration, this additional cost can be easily justified if the extended functional footprint and flexibility of the selected solution allows an enterprise to build a solution that can be quickly adapted to changing business needs.

The supply chain solution evaluation should always start with an elaborate list of business functions that are required to be supported by this new technology. These functions will list the existing processes, changes planned in the existing processes, future processes expected to be required to support known business goals, and best industry-wide practices that an enterprise may be thinking of adopting. This list should then be evaluated against the functions supported by the technology to identify the gaps. If the gaps are minor and do not impact any core process, the solution should be considered a good fit. However, if the gaps are many, impact core processes, or do not provide adequate flexibility for the business to evolve, then alternatives should be considered.

An example will further clarify the situation. Most companies investing in a transportation planning solution just a couple of years ago would not have considered multimodal support to be very critical to their operations. But volatile energy prices in the last two years have focused a lot of attention on this capability. Mixed modes using rail and road are definitely an alternative to consider for long-haul routes now, but such a change in business practices will not only require process and organizational changes, but also application and technology changes for a quick deployment. For an enterprise in this example, a qualitatively superior solution, even with the additional solution acquisition and deployment costs, would have paid off in a matter of weeks in the changed circumstances.

Software as a Service (SaaS) or License

Software as a service (SaaS) is a relatively new offering in the supply chain technology space. The model allows a corporation to buy the application services from the solution vendors without the need to host them on their own infrastructure. The application in this case is deployed and maintained by the solution vendor, and made available to customers via the Web. The SaaS model differs from the earlier application service provider (ASP) model in that these applications are designed from the ground up for deployment via the Web, and have a multi-tenant data model to simultaneously service many customers through a shared data model.

The alternative is the traditional licensing model, where a corporation must buy the software licenses and invest in hardware and other infrastructure to host its own solution for supporting the business functions.

The cost models in these two options vary widely. The SaaS model allows the corporations to benefit from a hosted application without the need for heavy upfront investments in technology, otherwise required in the conventional licensing model. However, the costs in the SaaS model are subscription based, and must be paid as long as the corporation needs that service. The traditional licensing model costs should drop over the years as the continuing costs have to pay only for maintenance and planned solution upgrades.

Not all business applications are suitable for SaaS-based delivery, but an increasing number of business applications are being offered as hosted services, including some of the supply chain applications like those for bid evaluations and transportation planning. While these and other supply chain applications may be available through this technology, an enterprise should consider the following before determining which model would likely be the best option:

- *Costs.* The cost models for the SaaS- and license-based models are different. Both models involve costs associated with evaluation of the solution scope, suitability, and vendor feasibility.

  The license-based models usually have large upfront costs for the software license and hardware. For SaaS-based applications, these up-front costs are quite negligible and generally would be limited to initial contract costs and any minimum subscription costs.

  Costs associated with the actual deployment also exist in both models. The licensed software approach will have additional tasks of installation, troubleshooting, and stabilization of the technology platform. Other costs related to consulting, modeling, integration, testing, configuration, and change management exist in both types of deployments, though the nature and extent of these costs will vary from one to the other.

  There are no transaction, business volume, or subscription-based costs in the traditional licensing model. All these costs can exist in the SaaS-based applications. In fact, these costs can add up quickly, especially for corporations that have large transaction volumes processed through such systems. For the SaaS solution providers, this provides the perpetual revenue flow.

  Finally, ongoing maintenance and upgrade costs can exist in both types of solutions, though the SaaS models are less likely to have such costs if the initial contract is well negotiated.

- *Solution scope and flexibility.* This is another important factor to consider in determining whether a SaaS- or license-based model would be better. While the initial evaluation of the solution to be able to support a corporation's processes is important, the ability to change the solution through configuration or customization to continuously support evolving business processes is equally important for organizational agility.

  As SaaS-based application models support many corporations simultaneously, their ability to customize the solution may be limited unless the changes are widely adopted in the industry. Such limitations can sometimes constrain an enterprise's ability to quickly change its business processes to react to market pressures.

  This flexibility will be especially important in those areas where an organization considers its business processes to be a definite competitive advantage for continued success.

- *Data.* Most of the software applications are data intensive. This is most true for the supply chain applications. By nature, these applications need large amounts of very sensitive data. For example, consider the sales forecasting function that requires historical sales at every location, for every product, along with the data on prices and promotions. This function also needs information on future assortments. Such data can be very sensitive for a retailer, and can be a competitive disadvantage if breached.

The SaaS models typically host the solutions and the data on common servers. If data privacy or security concerns exist, it would be prudent to consider license-based models for such processes.

- *Integration.* Systems integration with other enterprise applications is an important aspect of software deployment and its successful adoption in the enterprise. Such integration may involve using common synchronized master data and transaction integration through batch or message-based processes.

  For license-based software deployments, such integration is typically a completely internal affair. Most likely, all such data resides on the same corporate network, uses high-speed fiber connections with large bandwidth, does not require any encryption during transit, and the integration tools, data formats, and communication protocols are well understood, with ample resources with the required skills. All of these factors may make it simpler than the SaaS-based solution deployment, where many of the above assumptions will not hold.

  Whereas some of integration processes may be infrequent, such as master data synchronization, others that exchange transactions or update transaction statuses may be required to be implemented in a real-time fashion. Volume and frequency of such updates can pose practical problems for larger clients and must be evaluated for feasibility.

  For example, consider a retailer whose store inventory snapshots must be updated from all its stores and its entire assortment prior to the replenishment planning process. If the replenishment process runs daily, then store data updates and replenishment process execution may have a very small window during which both processes must finish. Such high-volume, high-frequency integration requirements should be adequately evaluated for all deployments, but more importantly for SaaS-based deployments due to their Web-based design.

  This also constrains the types of applications that are most compliant with the SaaS model and lend themselves easily to this type of deployment.

- *Service-level agreements.* Whereas the licensing corporation can have complete control over system availability and decide on planned maintenance windows to suit its operations, this may not always be the case for SaaS-based deployments. SaaS vendors have a large number of corporations as clients and may have system availability agreements that should be closely reviewed and understood to avoid surprises.

However, a large client base may also allow the SaaS-based vendors to invest in well-designed failover and high-availability systems to provide virtually uninterrupted service even during their planned maintenance windows.

- *Content.* Another consideration for what functions are generally more suitable for the SaaS-based model is the need for third-party business content for the business function.

  For example, consider the global trade management functions that require consistent updates of content such as blacklisted parties or customs duties for many jurisdictions worldwide. Such content updates are expensive as well as a compliance risk if not maintained properly. SaaS-based deployment with explicit service guarantees for up-to-date content may provide a good opportunity for leveraging this function as a service rather than a licensed application.

  Other examples where SaaS-based models in supply chains have become popular are transportation planning, bid evaluation and awards, and supplier evaluation and on-boarding.

- *Upgrades.* The solution provider's ability, willingness, and contractual obligation to keep the software up to date is an important factor. In the traditional license model, most corporations sign up for maintenance contracts with the software providers that allow them to upgrade their systems when new functionality becomes available, or when the support on the older systems is dropped. As the software vendors upgrade their solutions to align with industry best practices, licensed corporate users have the option to evaluate the new functionality and upgrade their systems at will.

  This may not be true for SaaS-based solution deployment, where such upgrade decisions may depend on the hosted solution provider and its other clients. Therefore, an informed qualification should be made before deploying SaaS-based software, to determine that it will not constrain the corporation from deploying industry best practices as they evolve or from adopting better business processes.

- *Contract cancellation.* This is a situation relevant only to SaaS-based software models. Most corporations do not put adequate thought into the exit strategy for these deployments. However, there are many reasons such a situation may arise, such as relationship with the vendor gone bad, increasing costs, better or less expensive solutions available elsewhere, change in organizational processes or priorities, or expansion of internal technology capabilities. When this happens, the corporation needs to make sure that it can legally retrieve all its business data from the vendor's current and archived databases, within a reasonable time, on specified media, with the option of ensuring that no copies of such data persist with the vendor. This is even more important when such data is of direct business value, or of a sensitive nature, such as sales projections or customer data. All other conditions for contract cancellation should be included along with clearly defined obligations for both the parties at the time of cancellation. Such terms help the partners cancel contracts prematurely if plans change, without any bitterness or professional jeopardy.

Such upfront planning on making such conditions part of the initial contract can also save time and difficulties at the time of cancellation. This affects the partner relationship positively, and allows the parties to continue their business relationship in other areas without distress.

Another important thing to plan is the transition of the business process to an alternative solution, which may be internal or external. In many cases, such a transition will require active help from the first solution vendor. This may involve getting the master and transaction data into the new system, running parallel systems while the new solution takes over, or transitioning partners from the old solution to the new. These activities should be identified, planned, and included in the service contract with the SaaS vendor.

Considerations for Successful Supply Chain Technology Deployments

There are many factors that affect successful technology deployments in general. Most of them are relevant to the discussion for supply chain applications in particular.

Master Data Management

Master data is the base data that provides the basic references to the organizational transactions. Examples of such data can be items, warehouses, stores, and virtual objects like account codes. Consistent use of such data provides a consistent context to the transactions so that these transactions can interact with each other, as well as consolidating for creating meaningful corporate-level metrics.

Consider a large retailer with many store brands that has some common assortments across these store brands. If the retailer wishes to determine the profitability of a specific product category across all its store brands, it will need to ensure that the product category is defined in the same way across these entities and that products have consistent reference so that they belong to the same category irrespective of the store chain selling them. Such a consistent reference will help the retailer to consolidate the costs as well as retail sales of this product and to correctly determine the profitability.

Master data management (MDM) refers to the collective processes for creating, collecting, cleansing and synchronizing, consolidating, validating, persisting, and publishing such data throughout the organization. These processes together ensure consistent reference data availability for usage across all enterprise systems and processes, and allow organizational control over continuing maintenance, update, and use of this data.

There are several solution options when it comes to master data management, including the solutions offered by the ERP vendors. If an enterprise already has an ERP solution from a specific vendor, then it should definitely evaluate the MDM solution offered by that vendor. Best-of-breed master data solution vendors may provide more flexible solutions that are built for a truly diverse technology landscape and may work better in situations where the IT landscape has multiple ERP, supply chain, and other business solutions.

Establishing MDM processes prior to deploying supply chain technologies substantially reduces risk, and enhances the probability of success in adopting and managing such technology. It ensures that all the supply chain processes can be integrated and automated in a systemic fashion, and performance metrics can be consistently defined, measured, and published to effect and manage desirable process and behavioral changes.

Process and Solution Alignment

Aligning the processes with the solution being deployed is a critical success factor for any technology deployment project. When a solution is custom developed to support a business function, it can be tailored to suit the process exactly as required. However, such solutions can become a liability when the underlying business process changes by constraining the business's ability to adapt.

Packaged solutions to support business functions have become more popular as an alternative to custom development. These solutions are generally more flexible as they are designed to be deployed across a large cross-section of business users. They may also provide best practice processes built into the technology solution. However, even the most flexible solutions will sometimes fall short of specific enterprise needs. In these cases, companies face the choice of changing the existing process to adopt the solution, or customizing the solution to support the existing process.

This is a trade-off that should not be taken lightly. While customizing the solution to suit the existing process is tempting, this can lead to higher deployment costs through design, development, and testing costs required for developing a custom solution, and higher maintenance costs through upgrades that require separate testing and debugging on such custom development. Ultimately, this can lead to technology obsolescence due to an enterprise's inability to upgrade its systems as technology changes. The alternative approach of changing the existing process may be cheaper unless the underlying business process provides a specific and quantifiable saving or a specific competitive advantage that the standard process supported by the vendor's solution does not provide.

Another alternative to manage solution customization is when the proposed changes make broad sense across the industry, and the solution provider can be persuaded to push these changes into the base solution. This can be mutually helpful, as the cost of development can be shared, and while the company benefits from the enhanced process support, the solution vendor also benefits from the enriched application footprint that makes it more competitive.

Partner Collaboration

As supply chain core functions primarily relate to planning and execution of material flows, they routinely involve external partners that an enterprise must deal with. The supply chain functions in most companies go through various stages of maturity concluding with the ability to actively collaborate with partners. The collaboration itself may further evolve from the simple ability to share information, to an interactive capability with automated decision-making systems that form the foundation of an adaptive supply chain.

Selecting technology solutions that are designed for such a collaborative approach would ensure that the path to supply chain maturity is not constrained due to technology limitations.

Solution capabilities for facilitating partner collaboration typically involve ability to define events, exceptions, alerts, automated messaging, rules, and workflows, in addition to the ability to address a distributed and diverse user group as per their roles and permissions to access applications and data.

As an example, a fully developed collaborative solution will allow a corporation to send purchase orders, and automatically react to the PO acknowledgments received from the vendor by acting on any deviations between the ordered and accepted quantities, through its replenishment planning applications. If the ordered quantity is 100, and the vendor confirms only 80, then the balance of 20 can be an input to the replenishment application to reconsider in its next iteration for order planning. Rules can be defined to automate such a resolution, or to alert a user for manual intervention where an automated resolution is not desirable.

The conventional supply chain technology solutions have been short on providing support for such an interactive and adaptive collaborative process. This is an emerging area with huge potential that is largely untapped by corporations as well as solution providers.

Technology Platform

Selecting a technology platform for the software solutions is an important task. While solution providers support many popular hardware platforms, the multiplicity of hardware platforms and other infrastructure such as operating systems, Web servers, app-servers, Web browsers, integration software, messaging software, security, and user management technologies makes it almost impossible to find a solution provider that is fully aligned with the enterprise technology standards. The abundance of open source code utilities, tendency of developers to use such utilities to shorten the development cycle, and lack of controls in the development environments only add to this complexity and the associated risk for liability due to unintended breaches of intellectual property and open source software agreements.

The determination of the technology platform, infrastructural software required to run an application, and other third-party business applications that may be embedded or required to be separately licensed to effectively use the main application all determine an organization's ability to adapt the technology and support it in the long term. This also affects the cost of maintenance of such technology.

The platform evaluation should also consider the ability of the platform technology to scale to the expected volumes and to perform to user expectations on response time, its flexibility on central or distributed deployment, its capability to have high-availability configuration for uninterrupted business support, and finally, the disaster recovery plans to safeguard and restart the critical business process support in case of disasters. Data and application security through restricted authenticated access, data encryption, data archiving and storing, and data backup characteristics are other considerations in the evaluation of technology.

Whereas companies spend a lot of time evaluating the functional scope and suitability of a business application, not many evaluate their ability to buy, deploy, and maintain the hardware and infrastructure required for the application. This can result in costly decisions or failed implementations.

Service-Oriented Architecture (SOA)

SOA is a relatively new development in software technology architecture. The SOA design philosophy is based on creating software that packages discrete business functions exposed as callable functions and then creating applications by combining these business function packages in a specific sequence. This allows a customizable framework for creating business applications by quickly rearranging these discrete packages. The closest physical analogy to SOA would be standard Lego® blocks that can be used to create many different shapes and sizes.

In an enterprise implementation of SOA-based applications, a central registry of services is deployed where all available business services are registered with their behaviors. Business analysts can then create applications by selecting these services. Think of the SOA registry as an enterprise-wide catalog of services where all available services are published. These services may be available only to applications within the corporate firewall, or may even be exposed for use by partners outside the corporate systems. An SOA repository complements the registry by providing a common place to keep all source code and design references for the published services.

When these SOA services are assembled together to build applications, they must communicate with each other, which is typically done through messages. These messages may be managed by a messaging server through an enterprise service bus (ESB). The ESB provides the infrastructure for receiving, routing, delivering, and sending back the acknowledgments for the messages.

Other concepts relevant to understanding and deploying SOA-based applications are workflow servers and the rules engine. These together control the flow of logic within the applications using the SOA services.

Whereas SOA has a lot of promise, any enterprise investing in SOA-enabled applications must establish some standards for services, registration, ownership, and maintenance. It is important to have services that are common to the enterprise across functions. To promote reusability, these services must be built with a design that can be extended as the service footprint grows to accommodate minor variations in the function execution. The ownership of such services that are common must be clearly identified, and the process by which this team will receive the inputs from the user teams and deliver more services should be well defined. It should be clearly understood that SOA introduces a lot of complexity into IT management and requires a clear strategy for technology planning and execution. A poorly thought-out SOA strategy that does not align the business requirements, technical requirements, and organizational processes is almost guaranteed to fail and create more issues than it solves.

Change Management

A lot has been written about the need to manage change associated with major technology deployments. This discussion is simply a reminder that all large technology deployments involve changes in processes that affect people who must cope with them for successful implementations.

Some of the common changes that accompany a supply chain technology deployment are mentioned below. Most of these are highly desirable changes and help in creating supply chain efficiencies that might have driven such projects in the first place. However, organizations routinely fail to recognize and plan for these changes until the changes start affecting the deployments.

Exception-Based Management

Most supply chain solutions leverage *exception-based management*. These solutions use data and user inputs to create plans and tasks that are then executed through a downstream process or through an ERP. Instead of pushing all such planned transactions for user review, these solutions typically allow users to define exception criteria, and then use these criteria to identify a small subset of these transactions for user review and input.

For example, a replenishment application making recommendations for creating purchase orders may be configured to process all purchase plans that are below a certain dollar value, and/or add a certain amount of inventory cover that is below the user-defined thresholds. The transactions that are within the defined thresholds will then be executed automatically by the purchase order management system, though these transactions will also be available for user review. The other transactions that did not meet these criteria due to higher dollar value or resulting inventory cover, will be held for user review and approval, before execution by the purchase order management system.

Exception-based management enhances process efficiency, and can result in labor savings due to the smaller number of buyers required to review all purchase transactions, but this requires a fundamental change in user behavior. Users and organizations must develop confidence in the solution's ability to react to daily demand changes and be able to let it automatically process purchases within the defined criteria. In fact, overriding the system recommendations may substantially undermine process effectiveness.

Such behavioral changes are hard to effect, take time, and most likely will require consistent management support and incentives to work. However, these are required changes without which the automation of many supply chain functions and their efficiencies can be undermined to the extent of making the whole investment questionable.

Organizational Metrics

Defining good success metrics to measure the successful implementation is another important part of managing change as a result of supply chain technology deployments. There are two categories of metrics that directly affect the success of such deployments.

The first group is the key performance indicators that measure improvements in process efficiencies. These are required to measure the impact of the deployment and compare this with projected improvements. For example, consider the order fulfillment rates for the sales orders after an inventory planning application has been deployed. Comparing the order fulfillment rates before and after the deployment will provide a good measure of the success of the new technology deployment. The process metrics are an obvious way to measure improvements, and are often a formal part of the implementation effort.

The second group of metrics is the group of key performance indicators that encourage adoption of the new technology by changing the metrics against which individuals' performance is measured and awarded. For example, consider a furniture retailer who has recently deployed a fulfillment system that allows it to fulfill customer delivery orders from the store nearest to the delivery address, rather than the store that captured the order. Before the deployment of this system, the store capturing the order also fulfilled the order and therefore received the full credit for the sale. This also constrained the retailer's ability to fulfill orders because if the selling store was out of inventory, then the sale could not be completed. The new process provides the retailer with the flexibility of accepting a customer order in a store even when the physical inventory in that store is out of the ordered item.

However, the new process requires that each store have visibility into other stores' inventory and delivery capacities and can create distribution orders on other stores for order fulfillment. This new process can improve the retailer's revenues and customer satisfaction. However, after the deployment, the first store gets all the sales credit, and the second store gets stuck with the cost of fulfillment. This leaves no incentive for the second store to fulfill the order. To create proper incentive for the second store to promptly fulfill such orders, the metrics for the store manager should be changed to reflect some part of the revenue generated through this order fulfillment. This kind of change management requires evaluating the existing organizational metrics for measuring people's performance in light of the changed process capabilities and determining whether they still represent the best alignment between the goals of the organization and those of an individual employee.

Alerts and Event Management

A large number of supply chain functions relate to execution and tracking of real-time processes. Shipping and distribution are good examples of such processes. Today's solutions allow users and managers to track these processes with real-time alerts that are triggered by the system when user-defined events occur along the lifecycle of a transaction. For example, when a shipment is picked up, an EDI message is sent from the carrier to the shipper. If the shipment pickup is delayed beyond a specified time after the planned pickup time, the system can detect this "delay event" and alert the user to it. These solutions allow users to define various such events and alerts. Some of these alerts can simply be for information, whereas others might require immediate user reaction. Current technologies make it possible for users to get such alerts on mobile devices and resolve them through specific workflows using the same devices. Workflows and rules can make such alert-driven processes even more effective as users can define elaborate decision tree–like structures so that relevant actions can be automated, or people can be informed. Unattended alerts can be raised in priority and forwarded for management's attention.

While such technologies help enterprises achieve higher efficiencies, users and managers must get used to this style of working and may sometimes find it intimidating in the beginning.

EDI, Messaging, and Partner On-boarding

EDI messages have become the standard language of business transactions among partners. Most supply chain deployments need some level of collaboration with partners that requires exchanging transactions. The most common examples for this type of interaction are the transportation and warehousing functions where transactions like shipment status messages, load tender, load tender response, and advance shipment notices can be interchanged through standardized EDI formats. These messages enable information exchange between systems belonging to different partners. The predefined format helps the receiving system to interpret the message and automatically take the required action or update the status of a transaction. This provides process-level integration among disparate systems and partners.

There are other methods as well to achieve similar process integration, through message-based interfaces that leverage other formats such as extensible markup language (XML) and provide a structured way to define and send messages across applications.

Successful supply chain technology makes use of such message-based process integration as it enables another level of process integration, making it more efficient, responsive, and less error prone. Some solutions have functionality to provide native support for accepting incoming EDI transactions without any processing, and also provide fully formatted outgoing EDI messages. Such capability reduces the deployment time and promotes standardized integration. However, such efforts can quickly fail to deliver for lack of a well-thought-out partner on-boarding program, which must be established to make sure that the carriers, vendors, customers, and any other internal or external partners can actually leverage the capability. On-boarding programs establish the list of target partners, messages, formats, and protocols to be used. They also should define a method for testing and validating the test message integration before a partner is brought onto the live systems. As all these activities require active involvement of the partner's technology teams, the on-boarding process may take longer than expected. However, successful partner on-boarding enhances the probability of successful solution implementation and ensures that the investments made in the technology actually pay for themselves through increased productivity. Many supply chain deployments fail to deliver, or take too long, simply because the process for partner on-boarding does not get enough attention and resources during the planning stages.

RFID Technology

R^{*FID (radio frequency identification) technology*} consists of a small embedded or printed electronic integrated circuit (called the *RF tag*) that can be encoded with desired information. When this RF tag is scanned by an RF reader, it sends the encoded information to the reader. This is essentially how a passive RF tag works. We will skip the rest of the discussion on RFID technology, types of RF tags, types of readers, tag attachment, tagging positions, and so on in favor of understanding the inventory management processes in the supply chain where use of RF tags can make the processes more efficient, accurate, or automated.

RF tags can be attached to an item, case, pallet, container, or shipping vehicle. As the inventory with RF tags moves through the supply chain, various readers positioned at strategic points in the supply chain can signal the status of the inventory in real-time.

For example, when the inventory leaves the manufacturer's warehouse, the *RFID readers* at the outbound docks can register the order and item information, triggering the shipping status for the order. When this shipment is received in the retailer's warehouse, the readers at the incoming dock not only change the order status to "received," but also read the exact quantity received, triggering the inventory receipt transaction in the warehouse. In this simple example, both warehouses can forgo manual scanning of the bar-codes on each pallet/license, making the process more efficient. RFID also has the potential of making the process more accurate by taking out the human element, where a receiving associate may actually have to scan a bar-code to get similar information. The RFID reader, on the other hand, simply reads the number of tags available as the shipment passes through the door, and can tell the exact quantity if each item is individually tagged, or if the case tag is properly coded.

The theoretical scope of use of RFID in supply chains is unlimited. If all items are assumed to be individually tagged with an RF tag, then in theory all receiving and shipments in the warehouse can be automated. A truck-mounted RFID reader can help in physical inventory counts, and correctly provide the on-hand inventory numbers that are otherwise almost never entirely accurate. The shelves in the stores can communicate with the inventory management system when the inventory falls below a certain predefined value. An automated checkout process can also be supported through RF tags when the buyer puts the merchandise in the cart and passes through the checkout lane equipped with the RFID reader.

All processes where inventory needs to be identified, counted, and compared can be automated to a large extent using RF tags. Many companies have started pilot programs using RFID, including some of the largest retail companies.

However, RFID has not yet delivered on its promises to the supply chain, and we will explore the likely reasons in the next section.

RFID Adoption in the Industry

RFID as a technology shows huge promise. This is one of those technologies that has the ability of overhauling the supply chains and changing our expectations completely. However, RFID adoption in the industry has been low. There are several possible reasons for the low adoption rates, though the most likely reasons are as follows:

- *Cost.* Cost of the RF tags has come down substantially but is still high for tagging every single item. But in addition to the absolute cost of the tags, cost sharing is a real concern in the industry. The most logical point for RF tag application is the manufacturer, though most benefits of the RF tags go to the downstream users, such as logistics providers and retailers. This produces a convoluted cost picture, where the manufacturers bear most of the costs and the downstream partners receive most of the benefits. Cost sharing is one of the current concerns that must be resolved before large-scale RFID adoption can be obtained.
- *Inaccuracies.* Accuracy of data as the RF tags are scanned is another major concern. With the commercially viable tags and readers, successful read rates have sometimes been claimed to be as low as 80%. More expensive tags and reading equipment do provide better accuracy, but unless these numbers approach close to 100%, the adoption in high-transaction inventory management functions may remain low. The low accuracy rates generate data inaccuracies that require manual overrides, which defeats the main benefit of RFID tagging.
- *Standardization.* Standardization of technology, as well as product identifiers, remains a major issue. The RF tag frequencies used in the United States are different from those in Europe and other countries, making the readers incompatible. The same is true for product

identifiers. Most of the current standards like UPC, GTIN, EAN, and so on are consistent across a region but have not been accepted widely across the globe.

- *Security and other concerns.* There are security concerns around data encryption and data interception. In theory, it is possible to clandestinely scan a passing container or trucks on the highway carrying RFID-enabled merchandise and obtain information on the contents of the shipment. Such scenarios need to be validated and secured to reduce the supply chain risks associated with pilferage, raids, and contamination.

APPENDIX C

Understanding Cross-docking

Supply chain management is all about *flows*. Material flowing through warehouses is no exception. Conventionally, warehouses were set up as inventory buffer points along the supply paths so that demand fluctuations across the network could be smoothed. That provided stability to the planning and operations of the supply chain.

But better technology, integrated systems, and near real-time information exchange have all made it possible now to operate warehouses more efficiently. Where the product and demand attributes allow, it is possible to leverage cross-docking opportunities and reduce the inventory buffers at the warehouses.

Cross-docking basically involves receiving the merchandise at the inbound docks and then shipping it out shortly after, without the need to stock it at the warehouse. If planned and executed properly, it saves the intermediate disposition, storage, and order fulfillment tasks in the warehouse. Well-planned cross-docking operations save resources across the board, at the warehouse (e.g., *labor, space,* and *equipment*) and also technology resources, by simplifying the process.

As cross-docking does not require the inventory to be stored at the warehouse, it provides dual advantages:

1. *Operational efficiency.* As the material does not have to be stored at the warehouse, and directly moves from the receiving docks to the shipping docks or staging areas, warehouse operations are more efficient.
2. *Inventory efficiency.* As the inventory moves directly from the receiving to the shipping docks, there is no storage at the warehouses for the cross-docked items, and that reduces total system inventory in the supply chain.

There are two variants of cross-docking that can be leveraged. Each addresses different situations and needs specific process/system capabilities, but both are founded in the cross-docking concept and provide the same advantages.

Planned Cross-docking or Flow-through

Planned cross-docking is a deliberate *strategy* for the supply chain. It consists of determining the products that will be the best candidates for cross-docking/flow-through operations, and then deploying a complete demand and supply management process that leverages the flow-through strategy at the warehouse. Products that are most desirable for such cross-docking typically show the following characteristics:

- Such products normally have consistent demand that is neither too high nor too low. They can be seasonal, as long as the seasonal demand has the same stable characteristics and the processes can handle seasonal data. The values of these attributes need to be established based on sales history data, averages, and speed of movement of specific merchandise. If the demand is too high, then the items may be best served with a direct-to-store distribution model; if the demand is too low or intermittent, then stocking such items at the distribution centers may be required to consistently meet service levels.
- They have good handling characteristics, though they may be conveyable or not. Flow-through operations may require staging, pallet-breaking, and repacking; and some products may just not have the physical characteristics conducive to such operations.

Once the target products have been determined, the implementation of the strategy requires that the supporting business processes are adjusted for making the shift. Some of these are discussed under Evaluating Readiness.

Opportunistic Cross-docking

This is an ad-hoc cross-docking process that takes advantage of real-time information exchanges among various distribution and fulfillment systems. Opportunistic cross-docking identifies when an inbound shipment or part of a shipment (LPN/pallet) can be used to fulfill an outstanding order by directly routing the inbound merchandise to the staging or shipping docks for an outbound order. Opportunistic cross-docking is typically a pure cross-docking exercise, and does not usually require any break-pallet or other similar intermediate tasks.

This type of cross-docking is not as process intrusive as the planned version. It is simpler to implement, and requires only that the warehouse systems have real-time visibility into all requirements, ongoing shipping and receiving activities, and yard inventory; and that they can react to such information dynamically. This means that the warehouses are using the RFID-based devices and processes, rather than paper-based processes.

Technically, most of the current systems are deployed in an integrated fashion, networked with other enterprise applications through messaging, and can exchange information in real-time, thus making this a reality. Therefore, this largely becomes a business decision rather than a technology decision.

Opportunistic cross-docking may not provide any significant inventory reduction benefits, though it is broadly applicable across most products and provides warehouse operational efficiencies without large changes in the business planning and execution processes.

Evaluating Readiness

If a corporation is ready to implement a flow-through strategy at the warehouses, it should make sure to review and plan through some of the following areas.

Warehouse Readiness

The physical assets in the warehouse, warehouse design, and layout affect the ability to implement a successful flow-through strategy.

Warehouses for cross-docking typically need a large number of dock doors and large areas devoted to staging. These warehouses can be seen to have two categories of products, "flow-through" and "stock-and-distribute." Depending on the proportion of the flow-through assortment compared to the total warehouse assortment, the areas required for staging and the number of dock doors will vary.

Flexible yard management processes are another requirement before a flow-through strategy can be successfully deployed. The warehouse system should have visibility into the inventory in the yard, as well as enough yard-jockeys to manage the trailers between the docks and the yard.

Mechanization can help. When large assortments at the warehouse are conveyable, mechanization helps simplify the flow of merchandise through the warehouse from the receiving docks to the staging areas or shipping docks. This is not a prerequisite but can have huge cost impacts if planned properly.

Business Readiness

Flow-through processes require changes in existing business processes and expectations.

A well-thought-out business process and an organization to identify and maintain the best candidates for flow-through should be established. There are certain products and demand characteristics that define the most desirable products for cross-dock type of replenishment. These characteristics can change over time (such as demand), and will require a review of the target assortment. The enterprise will clearly need to establish the criteria, frequency, and ownership for these processes. The inventory profiles of these products will vary as they move to the flow-through strategy. It is important to understand how such changes will affect the current inventory metrics and the team's perception of success.

Replenishment planning is the other business process that impacts the flow-through strategy. The process must consider that there is no longer any warehouse storage of these products. This may mean adjusting safety stocks at the stores, service-level expectations, and potentially the frequency and size of orders. Some of these changes may require renegotiating with the suppliers, and will add their own lead-time before these changes can be implemented.

The fulfillment network must be reviewed to make sure that all stores are within an acceptable distance from their primary distribution center. Flow-through strategy may result in smaller but more frequent shipments to stores. Make sure that the distribution network is capable of handling such changes without an adverse effect on the service levels.

Distribution operations at the warehouses will be affected when the warehouse task planning system reacts to real-time changes in receiving and shipment requests. As these dynamically scheduled operations will directly affect the warehouse associates, make sure that the people in the distribution center and the stores are aware of the intended changes, and have bought into the corporate strategy. Reevaluate old processes related to schedules and frequency of receiving in the stores, relative priority of shipments received from a distribution center over shipments from suppliers, store labor planning, and scheduling models. All these processes may need to be reviewed and validated for their alignment with the new strategy.

System Readiness

Finally, the enterprise systems must be ready to support the following changes in the business processes and operations:

- *Analytics*. Make sure that there is enough historical sales data and analytics capability to define the best targets for the flow-through strategy. The strategy is bound to fail if the targeted products do not have the characteristics defined previously.

- *Warehouse management.* Warehouse management systems will typically need to be integrated with the enterprise systems to receive real-time updates on shipments, material requests, and distribution orders. They should be able to react to these changes, and re-plan if required. A paper-based process in the warehouse cannot be used for dynamic changes in the plans, and therefore it must be ensured that the warehouse management system supports the wireless handheld terminals in the warehouses. A warehousing system that is integrated with automation/mechanization increases efficiencies and reduces errors.
- *Forecasting and replenishment.* Review the forecasting and replenishment processes to establish the level at which the forecasts and purchase orders are generated. Inventory planning systems that can dynamically compute the optimal inventory levels, and guarantee service levels, ensure a successful transition to the flow-through strategy. A collaborative environment for sharing orders and fulfillment plans with the suppliers can greatly help. Inventory visibility across the enterprise across all inventory-carrying locations is another useful tool to have. All these capabilities enhance the efficiency of the flow-through process. However, some of them are required and their absence will certainly hinder a successful implementation of the flow-through strategy.
- *Allocation.* A flow-through environment makes it possible to review the original allocations again at the time of receiving the merchandise. Though it is not required, it allows the retailers to react to any demand changes in the time between when the order was placed and when the merchandise is received. The concept is very similar to manufacturing industries holding off the final assembly to the last possible minute.

  If the retailer decides to reallocate the ordered merchandise at the time of receiving, then it must make sure that its allocation systems are capable of reviewing and reallocating merchandise on-demand.

  However, if the orders are left intact and shipped directly to the stores as ordered, then the warehouse and ordering systems should be reviewed to ensure that the order pegging is maintained between the distribution center and store orders.
- *Logistics.* Flow-through implementation may affect the characteristics of the shipments from the distribution centers to the stores. It is likely that the number of shipments will increase, with more multistop shipments and more frequent shipments. Ensure that the transportation systems can optimize such shipments, track them as they move, and allow changes by users if required.

Cross-docking or flow-through is definitely a strategy worth a serious review. However, a successful implementation requires that the people fully grasp the concept and plan vigorously for success.

Supply Chain and Finance: A Quick Primer

Corporations are economic entities. Most commercial corporations exist with a single motive: to productively engage in economic activity and create wealth for their investors and value for their customers and employees. The financial metrics measure the success of these corporations, and these are the numbers that are reported quarter after quarter to propel the engines of economy. Therefore, it is no surprise that most initiatives taken up by corporations are driven by a financial imperative.

Supply chain initiatives are no exception. Supply chain processes basically help the corporate finances in two ways:

1. They can reduce the *direct cost of operations* affecting their *cost of goods sold* (COGS). This means higher margins, reflected in the bottom line. An example in this category is reduction in distribution costs through enhanced transportation planning and execution processes. This is a direct savings that will simply result in increased margins given that all other factors remain the same.
2. They can make the operations more efficient, therefore reducing the *working capital* required to support these operations. By reducing the working capital required to support the operations, these supply chain functions increase the efficiency of deployed assets; this is reflected in increased asset turnover. An example in this category is lower inventories through better inventory planning, demand planning, and supply planning processes. Lower inventory levels mean less money invested in inventory, reducing the working capital required to run the company. Lower inventory levels result in higher inventory turns, which translates into higher asset turns.

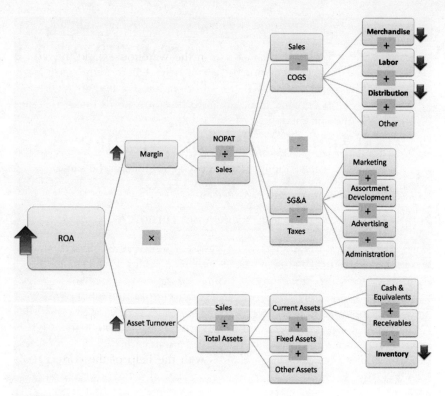

EXHIBIT D.1 Supply Chain and Finance

Exhibit D.1 shows how *return on assets (ROA)* is affected by supply chain initiatives.

Supply Chain Processes Reducing COGS

As shown in Exhibit D.1, three of the major COGS components for retailers are the cost of merchandise, distribution, and labor. Here is how supply chain initiatives can help reduce these costs:

1. *Merchandise.* These costs can be reduced through the strategic sourcing, bid optimization, and supplier contracts–based optimization. Good demand forecasting and supply management practices also help in reducing the cost of merchandise by reducing obsolescence and resulting merchandise clearance events.
2. *Distribution.* Distribution costs primarily consist of warehousing and transportation. Supply chain processes that can help reduce these

costs are network planning, warehouse management, and transportation management.

3. *Labor*. Labor costs for retailers are in the warehouses and the stores. Warehouse management processes can help directly reduce the labor costs in the warehouses, by better labor planning, scheduling, and task tracking. Better demand forecasting in the stores helps in streamlining the labor plans in the stores.

Any reduction in COGS directly translates into increased margins if the other factors (e.g., sales, administrative costs, etc.) remain the same.

Supply Chain Processes Increasing Asset Turnover

Asset turnover is a function of sales and total assets of a corporation. The inventory forms a substantial part of the total assets for a retailer. There are several supply chain processes that affect inventory and help reduce total inventory in the supply chain while maintaining the fulfillment or service levels to replenish the stores.

Better demand forecasting, inventory planning, and replenishment planning processes together help in reducing inventory in the system. Good demand and supply planning practices with the help of the correct tools have been shown to reduce inventories dramatically, though these systems sometimes require investment in technologies and skills that may not be available within the enterprise. Any reduction in inventory directly reduces the current assets and positively impacts the returns on assets.

Supply chain network optimization can also help reduce inventory levels by optimizing a network that is most efficient for replenishing the stores. This is a one-time benefit, and as the network of stores continues to grow, the supply network must be reevaluated to keep pace with the changes. However, frequent changes to the supply chain network are impractical due to heavy capital costs and long lead-times required to set up distribution centers.

APPENDIX E

How Green Is Your Supply Chain?

Finally, we say a few words on the "greenness" of the supply chain. Global warming has focused a lot of attention on the carbon footprint of a company's operations. Supply chains form a substantial part of that carbon footprint as they are used to plan, control, and execute the movement of goods across the corporation's supply chains.

There are quite a few opportunities within the scope of supply chain functions to review and reduce this footprint. But there are also issues outside the supply chain that need to be addressed at the corporate and strategic levels to create carbon-friendly supply chains. For example, the assortment decisions are typically outside the scope of the supply chain functions, but can affect sourcing and hence the carbon footprint of the supply chain.

For a corporation to truly "think green," an integrated view of strategy and operations must be taken. Reviewing all the processes from merchandise planning, assortment planning, and demand and supply planning to logistics and distribution from the green point of view can provide substantial insights into a corporation's footprint and generate enough suggestions to improve it.

Going green has its own cost and image benefits, and can be executed in a profitable manner. One of the current issues is that most corporations do not have a holistic view of the costs, and the total cost of merchandise on the shelf of the store is truly an unknown quantity. An integrated cost model for the enterprise can show the positive impact of selecting green strategies that are better for the environment and do not adversely affect the bottom line.

To this discussion, add the attempts at legislating the carbon emissions. Such legislation will almost certainly push up the prices of goods proportional to the distance between their points of production and consumption. That does not mean that the global trade will cease, just that an additional cost parameter will impact decisions for sourcing the merchandise. There is also talk of "carbon labeling" in the industry, which would require retailers not only to gather the information but also to share it with consumers. All these changes, legislative or otherwise, will drive the companies to review their existing processes and enhance them to align with the changes in the external environment.

Consider some of the organizational processes in retail that would impact the carbon footprint considerably if they were planned and executed differently.

Integrated Assortment Planning and Sourcing

The current assortment planning process is primarily a revenue-driven process. Assortment planning is very tightly integrated with merchandise financial planning, and therefore its primary objective is to drive the financial and revenue targets.

Assortment planning, however, determines what merchandise will be sold in which stores and channels. The decision is almost completely independent of supply chain and fulfillment logistics considerations

In the future, the two processes may work together toward directly optimizing the profitability rather than being focused on revenues. Such a process will have to take into account the cost of delivering the specific merchandise to that store/channel from the potential sources. It will also consider the cost of complying with local regulations, which may change regionally. The costs of recycling and returns may be modeled as well. The shift from revenue to profitability-driven assortment planning will certainly affect the assortments. It will drive more local assortments and will provide an integrated view of the sourcing and assortment plans.

Sourcing and Supplier Selection: Manufacturing, Packaging, and Recycling

Current retail processes do not explicitly consider the previously mentioned aspects of the merchandise sold. Most retailers have become aware of the manufacturing methods, and already consider this as part of their vendor selection process due to labor and environmental conditions in some of the developing countries where such factories are located. But this consideration is largely limited to the labor conditions and focused on avoiding any negative brand publicity. The price and quality of the manufactured merchandise is still the major common driver in making sourcing decisions.

So, how should the approach for sourcing evolve for a carbon-aware supply chain corporation?

A *carbon-aware supply chain* requires that the sourcing decisions and vendor approval processes get extended to consider the extended aspects of the manufacturing process. Instead of limiting the assessment to its ability to produce defect-free merchandise at an acceptable price, the process would also consider the following:

- Assess the technology used for energy efficiency by considering things such as the level of automation, type of automation, fuel used, and energy efficiency of the process.
- Assess packaging material used, amount and value of packaging compared to the value of the core merchandise, recycling attributes of the packaging materials, presence or absence of recycling facilities for packaging at the place of consumption, and local regulations governing recycling and disposal of material involved. If recycling facilities do not exist in the destination regions, will the retailer provide collection points/services for packaging material? Can this be sent back directly to the manufacturer or its agent? Such considerations will need to become more commonplace and a standard part of the sourcing assessments.

Logistics and Distribution

The logistics and distribution processes cover the warehousing and transporting of merchandise from the suppliers to the stores. These are by far the most obvious processes for carbon-aware supply chain planning. As legislative pressures push retailers to measure and report the carbon impact of their supply chain activities, it will become necessary for the retailers to improve their logistics and distribution processes, enhance efficiencies, and reduce the related costs.

Transportation optimization will become widely adopted to reduce the total mileage to ship merchandise worldwide. Collaborative shipping (co-shipping) may become more popular to share the costs and reduce the carbon footprint where possible.

Supply chain flow-path optimization may become one of the more popular applications with more frequent evaluation of the flow-paths for merchandise. Retailers may adopt more flexible processes where merchandise can dynamically change flow-paths to serve immediate demand, leverage cross-docking, and directly ship to stores to optimize the mileage.

Total Landed Cost

While most retailers struggle with the collection and maintenance of total landed costs today, it will be the single most important piece of information to determine the carbon costs of the supply chain.

The cost of goods sold consists of many parts. Some of these costs are direct costs that are easy to capture and measure accurately, such as the cost of purchasing the merchandise from the supplier. Other costs are indirect and a little harder to accurately allocate, but these are still available with a large degree of reliability, such as warehousing costs for storage and handling of inventory. Finally, there are the indirect costs of the supporting processes, which may be hardest to measure and account for; examples of such costs are the cost of planning, forecasting, ordering, or of maintenance of the technology infrastructure *specifically* supporting a given supply chain process. Green supply chains may have additional cost elements like the cost of providing recycling facilities, cost of collecting additional data on merchandise and packaging characteristics, and so on. Ability to measure, evaluate, and analyze the cost information accurately can help retailers identify their most profitable merchandise categories and prioritize their efforts on their most inefficient processes.

While packaged applications for capturing and reporting the total landed costs are not very prevalent today, they will emerge and support the effort to optimize the carbon-aware supply chain.

Depth of Supply Chain Models

By the *depth* of supply chain models, we mean the number of *vertical* supply chain echelons modeled for planning purposes. As carbon costs become a significant planning driver, retail supply chains will not stop at the supplier, but may have to include their supplier's suppliers as well. These deeper supply chain models will have the ability to model the parameters affecting the carbon footprint, and allow retailers to make strategic decisions that will support their execution plans and targets for carbon costs.

Carbon Cost Index

A carbon cost index may evolve to model and support the industry's effort to measure and control the carbon footprint and related costs, legislative or otherwise. Please note that these are *likely* scenarios presented here as mere possibilities to measure, impact, and control the carbon footprints of supply chains, and not *existing* requirements. These measures might evolve in ways quite different from those presented here.

Such a carbon cost index might model the following attributes of supply chains:

- *Energy profile*. The energy profile will model the total energy requirements of producing the raw materials as well as the manufacturing process that converts them into finished merchandise. Such data typically will be supplied by the manufacturers, through a process very similar to the product specifications that the manufacturers provide today. The existing data pools like GDSN may be expanded to include this data for the energy profiles of the manufacturing process and the energy profiles of the raw materials.

- *Recycle profile.* This profile will model the material's recycling characteristics, types of facilities required, and regional laws governing recycling requirements by collecting data on the recycling profiles for the merchandise as well as for the packaging materials.

- *Distribution profile.* This will capture the carbon footprint of the material movements required to manufacture a given product, with elements such as the distances traveled by the raw materials from their source to the factories, and by the finished goods to reach the retailer's warehouses and stores from the factories. The modes available on these routes and energy profiles of these modes may affect such scores. It might also capture the distribution unit profile, which might affect distribution costs.

Once defined, the carbon cost index may be used in several planning and optimization functions for the supply chain processes.

Commonly Used EDI Transaction Codes

The following is a list of commonly used EDI transaction sets for easy reference. These have been compiled from a more exhaustive list available at www.1edisource.com.

- 104 Air Shipment Information
- 106 Motor Carrier Rate Proposal
- 107 Request for Motor Carrier Rate Proposal
- 108 Response to a Motor Carrier Rate Proposal
- 110 Air Freight Details and Invoice
- 114 Air Shipment Status Message
- 204 Motor Carrier Load Tender
- 210 Motor Carrier Freight Details and Invoice
- 211 Motor Carrier Bill of Lading
- 213 Motor Carrier Shipment Status Inquiry
- 214 Transportation Carrier Shipment Status Message
- 215 Motor Carrier Pickup Manifest
- 216 Motor Carrier Shipment Pickup Notification
- 217 Motor Carrier Loading and Route Guide
- 218 Motor Carrier Tariff Information
- 224 Motor Carrier Summary Freight Bill Manifest
- 300 Reservation (Booking Request) (Ocean)
- 301 Confirmation (Ocean)
- 303 Booking Cancellation (Ocean)
- 304 Shipping Instructions
- 309 Customs Manifest
- 310 Freight Receipt and Invoice (Ocean)
- 312 Arrival Notice (Ocean)
- 313 Shipment Status Inquiry (Ocean)
- 315 Status Details (Ocean)

- 323 Vessel Schedule and Itinerary (Ocean)
- 326 Consignment Summary List
- 350 Customs Status Information
- 352 U.S. Customs Carrier General Order Status
- 353 Customs Events Advisory Details
- 354 U.S. Customs Automated Manifest Archive Status
- 355 U.S. Customs Acceptance/Rejection
- 356 U.S. Customs Permit to Transfer Request
- 357 U.S. Customs In-Bond Information
- 404 Rail Carrier Shipment Information
- 410 Rail Carrier Freight Details and Invoice
- 601 U.S. Customs Export Shipment Information
- 753 Request for Routing Instructions
- 754 Routing Instructions
- 810 Invoice
- 812 Credit/Debit Adjustment
- 820 Payment Order/Remittance Advice
- 840 Request for Quotation
- 843 Response to Request for Quotation
- 846 Inventory Inquiry/Advice
- 850 Purchase Order
- 853 Routing and Carrier Instruction
- 855 Purchase Order Acknowledgment
- 856 Ship Notice/Manifest
- 860 Purchase Order Change Request—Buyer Initiated
- 865 Purchase Order Change Acknowledgment/Request—Seller Initiated
- 869 Order Status Inquiry
- 870 Order Status Report
- 990 Response to a Load Tender

Incoterms (International Commercial Terms)

Incoterms[1] are a set of trading terms that have been standardized for international trade and are widely accepted. These terms identify the respective responsibilities of the buyer and the seller for international trade, and the party responsible for bearing the costs involved. Incoterms are used with a geographical location and do not deal with transfer of title.

Incoterms are published by the ICC (International Chamber of Commerce), and have been reproduced as such.

Group E—Departure:

- *EXW*. Ex Works (named place): "Ex works" means that the seller delivers when he places the goods at the disposal of the buyer at the seller's premises or another named place (i.e., works, factory, warehouse, etc.) not cleared for export and not loaded on any collecting vehicle.

  This term thus represents the minimum obligation for the seller, and the buyer has to bear all costs and risks involved in taking the goods from the seller's premises.

  However, if the parties wish the seller to be responsible for the loading of the goods on departure and to bear the risks and all the costs of such loading, this should be made clear by adding explicit wording to this effect in the contract of sale. This term should not be used when the buyer cannot carry out the export formalities directly or indirectly. In such circumstances, the FCA term should be used, provided the seller agrees that he will load at his cost and risk.

---

[1]Incoterms 2000™ & ®: Incoterms is a trademark of ICC, registered in the European Community and elsewhere. ICC Publication N° 560 (E)—ISBN 92.842.1199.9. Published in its official English version by the International Chamber of Commerce, Paris. Copyright © 1999—International Chamber of Commerce (ICC). Available from ICC Services SAS, 38 cours Albert 1er, 75008 Paris, France and www.iccbooks.com.

Group F—Main Carriage Unpaid:

- *FCA*. Free Carrier (named place): "Free Carrier" means that the seller delivers the goods, cleared for export, to the carrier nominated by the buyer at the named place. It should be noted that the chosen place of delivery has an impact on the obligations of loading and unloading the goods at that place. If delivery occurs at the seller's premises, the seller is responsible for loading. If delivery occurs at any other place, the seller is not responsible for unloading.

  This term may be used irrespective of the mode of transport, including multimodal transport. "Carrier" means any person who, in the contract of carriage, undertakes to perform or to procure the performance of transport by rail, road, air, sea, inland waterway, or by a combination of such modes.

  If the buyer nominates a person other than the carrier to receive the goods, the seller is deemed to have fulfilled his obligation to deliver the goods when they are delivered to that person.

- *FAS*. Free Alongside Ship (named port of shipment): "Free Alongside Ship" means that the seller delivers when the goods are placed alongside the vessel at the named port of shipment. This means that the buyer has to bear all the costs and risks of loss of or damage to the goods from that moment.

  The FAS term requires the seller to clear the goods for export.

  THIS IS A REVERSAL FROM THE PREVIOUS INCOTERMS VERSIONS WHICH REQUIRED THE BUYER TO ARRANGE FOR EXPORT CLEARANCE.

  However, if the parties wish the buyer to clear the goods for export, this should be made clear by adding explicit wording to this effect in the contract of sale.

  This term can be used only for sea or inland waterway transport.

- *FOB*. Free On Board (named port of shipment): "Free On Board" means that the seller delivers when the goods pass the ship's rail at the named port of shipment. This means that the buyer has to bear all the costs and risks of loss of or damage to the goods from that point. The FOB term requires the seller to clear the goods for export. This term can be used only for sea or inland waterway transport. If the parties do not intend to deliver the goods across the ship's rail, the FCA term should be used.

Group C—Main Carriage Paid:

- *CFR*. Cost and Freight (named port of destination): "Cost and Freight" means that the seller delivers when the goods pass the ship's rail in the port of shipment.

The seller must pay the cost and freight necessary to bring the goods to the named port of destination, BUT the risk of loss of or damage to the goods, as well as any additional costs due to events occurring after the time of delivery, are transferred from the seller to the buyer.

The CFR term requires the seller to clear the goods for export. This term can be used only for sea or inland waterway transport. If the parties do not intend to deliver the goods across the ship's rail, the CPT term should be used.

■ *CIF*. Cost, Insurance and Freight (named port of destination): "Cost, Insurance and Freight" means that the seller delivers when the goods pass the ship's rail in the port of shipment.

The seller must pay the cost and freight necessary to bring the goods to the named port of destination, BUT the risk of loss of or damage to the goods, as well as any additional costs due to events occurring after the time of delivery, are transferred from the seller to the buyer. However, in CIF the seller also has to procure marine insurance against the buyer's risk of loss of or damage to the goods during the carriage.

Consequently, the seller contracts for insurance and pays the insurance premium. The buyer should note that under the CIF term the seller is required to obtain insurance only on minimum cover. Should the buyer wish to have the protection of greater cover, he would either need to agree as much expressly with the seller or to make his own extra insurance arrangements.

The CIF term requires the seller to clear the goods for export. This term can be used only for sea or inland waterway transport. If the parties do not intend to deliver the goods across the ship's rail, the CIP term should be used.

■ *CPT*. Carriage Paid To (named place of destination): "Carriage paid to ..." means that the seller delivers the goods to the carrier nominated by him, but the seller must in addition pay the cost of carriage necessary to bring the goods to the named destination. This means that the buyer bears all risks and any other costs occurring after the goods have been delivered.

"Carrier" means any person who, in the contract of carriage, undertakes to perform or to procure the performance of transport by rail, road, air, sea, inland waterway, or by a combination of such modes.

If subsequent carriers are used for the carriage to the agreed destination, the risk passes when the goods have been delivered to the first carrier.

The CPT term requires the seller to clear the goods for export. This term may be used irrespective of the mode of transport including multimodal transport.

- *CIP*. Carriage and Insurance Paid to (named place of destination): "Carriage and Insurance paid to . . ." means that the seller delivers the goods to the carrier nominated by him, but the seller must in addition pay the cost of carriage necessary to bring the goods to the named destination. This means that the buyer bears all risks and any other costs occurring after the goods have been so delivered. However, in CIP the seller also has to procure insurance against the buyer's risk of loss of or damage to the goods during the carriage. Consequently, the seller contracts for insurance and pays the insurance premium.

  The buyer should note that under the CIP term the seller is required to obtain insurance only on minimum cover. Should the buyer wish to have the protection of greater cover, he would either need to agree as much expressly with the seller or to make his own extra insurance arrangements.

  "Carrier" means any person who, in the contract of carriage, undertakes to perform or to procure the performance of transport by rail, road, air, sea, inland waterway, or by a combination of such modes.

  If subsequent carriers are used for the carriage to the agreed destination, the risk passes when the goods have been delivered to the first carrier.

  The CIP term requires the seller to clear the goods for export. This term may be used irrespective of the mode of transport including multimodal transport.

Group D—Arrival:

- *DAF*. Delivered at Frontier (named place): "Delivered at Frontier" means that the seller delivers when the goods are placed at the disposal of the buyer on the arriving means of transport not unloaded, cleared for export, but not cleared for import at the named point and place at the frontier, but before the customs border of the adjoining country. The term "frontier" may be used for any frontier including that of the country of export. Therefore, it is of vital importance that the frontier in question be defined precisely by always naming the point and place in the term.

  However, if the parties wish the seller to be responsible for the unloading of goods from the arriving means of transport and to bear the risks and costs of unloading, this should be made clear by adding explicit wording to this effect in the contract of sale.

  This term may be used irrespective of the mode of transport when goods are to be delivered at a land frontier. When delivery is to take place in the port of destination, on board a vessel or on quay (wharf), the DES or DEQ terms should be used.

- *DES*. Delivered Ex Ship (named port of destination): "Delivered Ex Ship" means that the seller delivers when the goods are placed at the disposal of the buyer on board the ship not cleared for import at the named port of destination. The seller has to bear all costs and risks involved in bringing the goods to the named port of destination before discharging. If the parties wish the seller to bear the costs and risks of discharging the goods, then the DEQ term should be used.

  This term may be used only when the goods are to be delivered by sea or inland waterway or multimodal transport on a vessel in the port of destination.

- *DEQ*. Delivered Ex Quay (named port of destination): "Delivered Ex Quay" means that the seller delivers when the goods are placed at the disposal of the buyer not cleared for import on the quay (wharf) at the named port of destination. The seller has to bear all costs and risks involved in bringing the goods to the named port of destination and discharging the goods on the quay (wharf). The DEQ term requires the buyer to clear the goods for import and to pay for all formalities, duties, taxes and other charges upon import.

  THIS IS A REVERSAL FROM THE PREVIOUS INCOTERMS VERSIONS WHICH REQUIRED THE SELLER TO ARRANGE FOR IMPORT CLEARANCE.

  If the parties wish to include in the seller's obligations all or part of the costs payable upon import of the goods, this should be made clear by adding explicit wording to this effect in the contract of sale.

  This term can be used only when the goods are to be delivered by sea or inland waterway or multimodal transport on discharging from a vessel onto the quay (wharf) in the port of destination. However, if the parties wish to include in the seller's obligations the risks and costs of the handling of the goods from the quay to another place (warehouse, terminal, transport station, etc.) in or outside the port, the DDU or DDP terms should be used.

- *DDU*. Delivered Duty Unpaid (named place of destination): "Delivered Duty Unpaid" means that the seller delivers the goods to the buyer, not cleared for import, and not unloaded from any arriving means of transport at the named place of destination. The seller has to bear the costs and risks involved in bringing the goods thereto, other than, where applicable, any "duty" (which term includes the responsibility for and the risks of the carrying out of customs formalities and the payment of formalities, customs duties, taxes, and other charges) for import in the country of destination. Such "duty" has to be borne by the buyer as well as any costs and risks caused by his failure to clear the goods for import in time.

However, if the parties wish the seller to carry out customs formalities and bear the costs and risks resulting therefrom as well as some of the costs payable upon import of goods, this should be made clear by adding explicit wording to this effect in the contract of sale.

This term may be used irrespective of the mode of transport but when delivery is to take place in the port of destination on board the vessel or on the quay (wharf), the DES or DEQ terms should be used.

- *DDP*. Delivered Duty Paid (named place of destination): "Delivered Duty Paid" means that the seller delivers the goods to the buyer, cleared for import, and not unloaded from any arriving means of transport at the named place of destination. The seller has to bear all the costs and risks involved in bringing the goods thereto including, where applicable, any "duty" (which term includes the responsibility for and the risks of the carrying out of customs formalities and the payment of formalities, customs duties, taxes, and other charges) for import in the country of destination.

Whilst the EXW term represents the minimum obligation for the seller, DDP represents the maximum obligation.

This term should not be used if the seller is unable directly or indirectly to obtain the import license.

However, if the parties wish to exclude from the seller's obligations some of the costs payable upon import of the goods (such as value-added tax: VAT), this should be made clear by adding explicit wording to this effect in the contract of sale.

If the parties wish the buyer to bear all risks and costs of the import, the DDU term should be used.

This term may be used irrespective of the mode of transport but when delivery is to take place in the port of destination on board the vessel or on the quay (wharf), the DES or DEQ terms should be used.

Index